W9-DDR-638

7 Keys to *Love*

Opening Love's Door to Joy & Wellbeing

2/2011

Dear Lynn,
Share the Love!

Sanford Hinden

WHOLE EARTH *Arts*

Copyright © 2009 by Sanford Hinden

All rights reserved, including the right to reproduce this work
in any form whatsoever, without permission in writing from
the publisher, except for brief passages with acknowledgment.

Cover design by Kim Kreischer and Gary Rosenberg
Cover art copyright © 2009 by Sanford Hinden
Interior design and production by Gary Rosenberg

Whole Earth ARTS, Inc.
131 East 24th Street
Huntington Station, NY 11746

If you are unable to order this book from your local bookseller,
you may order directly online at www.7keystolove.net

Library of Congress Control Number 1-234064264
2009 / 7 Keys to Love / Sanford Hinden, 1946

ISBN: 978-0-9841679-0-6
0-9841679-0-0

Contents

*Awakening
the sleeping love
of the world . . .*

All life
is a manifestation of the spirit,
the manifestation of love.

Each and every master, regardless of the era or the place,
heard the call and attained harmony with heaven and earth.
There are many paths leading to the top of Mount Fuji,
but there is only one summit-love.

Economy is the basis of society.
When the economy is stable, society develops.
The ideal economy combines the spiritual and the material,
and the best commodities to trade in are sincerity and love.

If your heart is large enough to envelop your adversaries,
you can see right through them and avoid their attacks.
And, once you envelop them, you will be able to guide them
along the path indicated to you by heaven and earth.

—MORIHEI UESHIBA, FOUNDER OF AIKIDO

Acknowledgments

My grateful acknowledgements to: My parents, Yetta and Joseph Hinden, for their belief in me, and for their love for their family and community; my son, Joseph, for his love for life and music and his wonderful sense of humor; Joie Hinden for her love for creativity; and Barbara and Dr. Robert Muller for ongoing creative inspiration and devotion to global love. To Dr Stanley Cohen, Pat Schmidt, and Marty Cohen for creative support and Kim Kreischer for her amazing art work.

To all the faculty and staff of Five Towns College for their daily creativity and love. To Diane and Steve Hinden for their support and love; Jo-Ann Hertzman for her abiding love and friendship; and Min. Thomas Humphrey and all the men and women supporters of the Long Island Men's Center for their inspiration, love, and courage to better the lives of all men, women, children, and families on Long Island.

To my co-creative, collaborative, loving, supportive friends around the world: Rev. Faridi McFree and the Heartoons; Dr. Peter van den Dungen and the International Network of

Museums for Peace; Edward Winchester, the Peace Makers Institute; Dr. Diane Rousseau and the Institute for Spiritual Sciences; Suzanne Riordan and Families Advocating for Compassionate Treatment; Lance White Magpie and The Lakota Foundation; Edward Dabrowski and Children's Mother Earth Gardens; Cedric Rose for believing in WholeEarthARTS; David Amram for being a creative genius, a loving man, and the father of world music, which I love.

Appreciation to Gary Rosenberg for planning and formatting the book beautifully and Karen Anspach for editing gracefully. Thanks also to all my creative friends and colleagues locally and globally who perform and work tirelessly to make the show go on, serve the community, and make the world a better place.

And, thanks to the creative universe and nature, all my relations, the two-legged, four-legged, winged, finned, and imagined. My love and appreciation to you all, always.

And love to my beloved.

Foreword

This book, 7 *Keys to Love,* took thirty years to write. I remember when Sandy Hinden showed me his manuscript of 800 pages of his collection of quotes on love in 1978. I referred him to my literary agent, who told Sandy it would be too expensive to publish in that format. Ten years later, Sandy proceeded to rewrite *Love's Journey,* as he called it then, and again twenty years later in this current form. It is a book that will show the people of the world why love is so important as a process for personal and global transformation. The world and humanity have always needed love and need love more now than ever.

As a former Assistant Secretary-General, and Cofounder and Chancellor of the United Nations University for Peace in Costa Rica, Sandy would write to me and we would exchange ideas and encouragement. Sandy is a very exceptional human being, entirely devoted to a better, ideal world. I have known him for more than thirty years. He constantly inspired me for my work and efforts at the United Nations. He had ceaseless great ideas and encouraged me to not give up. He once collected the epithets given to me over the years by various people and institutions, and I once submitted an application for him to work at the United

Nations and believed he would have been precious capital for philanthropic organizations or for a major newspaper. I would have been so happy see him in charge of a major newspaper section on good news and happiness for the people. He would have been very precious for a major philanthropic organization, especially one dealing with internationally problems. I am happy he continues to create projects for humankind and does workshops to facilitate human beings becoming the most they can be individually, and as creative and loving partners and couples.

I hope every teacher in the world will read *7 Keys to Love*. It is the textbook for teaching children and parents how to create *Paradise Earth*, which I firmly believe is possible on our magnificent planet so blessed with beauty and life in this vast and wondrous universe. Sandy Hinden has been my devoted friend for thirty years. What a wonderful, loving friend he has been. I am so happy he now shares loves' journey with you as *7 Keys to Love*. I hope everyone in the United Nations will read this book.

—Robert Muller

In my work as a global public relations consultant, working closely with business, nonprofit organizations, governments and the United Nations, I can say that no one on this planet is more efficient or works harder than Sandy Hinden, for his causes and his clients. Whoever has him on their team is indeed fortunate as he creates and inspires miracles for their dream and cause.

When I read this manuscript of *7 Keys to Love* I thought it was excellent, and I encouraged Sandy to publish the book. As a past President of the Book Publicists in California, I saw that *7 Keys to Love* would be the next a hot topic after Eckhart Tolle's book *A*

New Earth. I thought this book would be great for Oprah's audience to read. On page 72 of *A New Earth—Awakening to Your Life's Purpose,* Eckhart Tolle says: ". . . all your actions and relationships will reflect the oneness with all life that you sense deep within. This is love. Laws, commandments, rules and regulations are necessary for those who are cut off from who they are, the Truth within. . . ." And, "Love and do what you will," says St. Augustine. Words cannot get much closer to the Truth than that. Love is the answer and yes, Sandy won't let us forget that. As an Advisory Board Member of the beautiful La Casa de Maria Retreat Center in Santa Barbara, I see his *Communications Skills for Conscious Partners & Couples Workshop* that includes *7 Keys to Love* as a must for all.

I knew about Sandy since I met Robert in 1994. I remember Robert speaking about him and meeting him at the United Nations for Robert's press conference and book signing. I met him again when he came from New York to visit us in Santa Barbara. He created a graphic for Robert's eighty-fourth birthday that was so beautiful. We were thrilled to see it as it had so many elements of Robert's sixty-year United Nations career woven together, including working closely with Secretary-Generals Dag Hammarskjold and U-Thant, whose pictures are in the graphic. Sandy, and his son Joseph were at the bottom of the graphic sharing their love for Robert. And now dear readers, you too will experience a new depth of love when you read *7 Keys to Love.*

—Barbara Gaughen Muller

Introduction

7 Keys to Love is a book for those interested in having a more love-filled life. It will most appeal to anyone seeking a healthy, loving relationship and to couples wishing to enhance their love life with their beloved. It will be of special interest to parents, teachers, clergy, religious educators, psychologists, social workers, youth counselors, health educators, workshop leaders, human resource trainers, wellness enthusiasts, mediators, politicians, elected officials, government policy makers with vision, and their aides.

7 Keys to Love is about the process of healing the heart; the power of seven keys to love in the individual, interpersonally and socially; and the process of helping the world though love, as has been hoped for by the religions of the world for thousands of years. The book presents, in easy to understand language, why we need love, why we enjoy it so much, and how we can use it to transform ourselves, each other, and the whole world. Although we think love is natural and simple, it actually can be enhanced with *love awareness* and practicing the *Seven Keys to Love*. This book will explore the rooms of the heart and the treasures that can be found within and between people able to express the many facets of love.

Why Is There a Need for *7 Keys to Love?*

There is a great need for *7 Keys to Love* because of our disconnection from each other. Violence of all kinds—domestic, community, and international—are caused by cycles of love denied, hurt, frustration, fear, and rage. When we gain greater awareness of the power of their opposites—appreciation, trust, forgiveness, tolerance, compassion, and loving-kindness—we can foster them. When we increase the skills of love—compassionate communication, empathy, collaboration, and synergy in everyday life—we have a chance of creating the world we really want: a paradise earth, a heaven on earth. *7 Keys to Love* clearly shows how the seven facets of love can enrich one's life and be the basis for a new, more conscious and loving society and world.

What Brought Me to the *7 Keys to Love?*

The awareness of the beauty, value, and need for love has grown in me over thirty years as I have helped dozens of projects and organizations and thousands of individuals grow and develop locally, nationally, and globally in the areas of health and human services, education, peace, the environment, and the arts.

I began helping people in the community over thirty years ago after receiving a bachelor of psychology degree from Queens College, City University of New York. I quickly realized the power of love to bring people together, heal their broken hearts, and empower them. I then researched the subject of love and compiled 800 pages of quotations and images about the many facets of love that I called *Love's Journey.* At this point in my journey of the heart I met an extraordinary man, Robert Muller, at a speech he gave at Fr. Thomas Berry's Riverdale Center for Religious Research in Riverdale, New York. Tom Berry was director of the graduate program in the History of Religions at Fordham University (1966–1979) and was president of the American Teilhard Association (1975–1987). He preferred to be described as a cosmologist, geologian, or "earth scholar," and advocated for deep ecology and "ecospirituality."

The extraordinary Robert Muller was the guest speaker on the *Future of Humankind*. He was an Assistant Secretary-General for the United Nations. He went on to have a sixty-year career at the UN, working closely with four Secretary-Generals. He started twenty-two specialized UN agencies and became the cofounder, and is now Chancellor Emeritus of the UN University for Peace. Robert became a mentor and dear friend. After he created the UN University for Peace in Costa Rica fifteen years ago, I told him, "Now we need an International Association for the Study of Love." He told me in his bold voice with his Alsace-Lorraine accent, "So, go do it!! And we need a University for Love." He and his wonderful wife Barbara Gaughen Muller have agreed to become honorary cochairpersons of the University for Love we will create. I am indebted to Barbara and Robert Muller (www. robertmuller.org) for being my mentors. They are two of the most devoted people in the world, to each other and to the planet. Robert wrote *Most of All They Taught Me Happiness*, and his latest book is *Paradise Earth*. I am so grateful to them for having written the preface to *7 Keys to Love*.

Inner Happiness and Inner Love

Each generation has to learn that happiness is an inside job—that we create our own happiness through our attitude, the meaning we assign to each situation, and how we respond to life's opportunities and challenges. We also need to realize that love starts from the inside, with consciously chosen self-love, and works its way outward into our world, to our friends, family, colleagues, and all the people we meet.

Nothing can stop the man with the right mental
attitude . . .nothing on earth can help the man
with the wrong mental attitude.

—THOMAS JEFFERSON

Most people are as happy
as they make up their minds to be.

—ABRAHAM LINCOLN

Today, make the decision to love everyone unconditionally.
Look at their best parts and focus only on that.
Truly love them and pay attention to
the results in your day.

—YEHUDA BERG

The Happiness-Love Attitude

Like happiness, many people do not feel love every day, even within long-term relationships. The feeling most of us want is the *happy glow of love*. This can actually be facilitated when the self honors and cherishes itself, not narcissistically, but with compassion and forgiveness for self and others. Ultimately, we want to be loved and adored by someone we love and adore. This can only happen if you make a conscious choice to love and allow yourself to be loved.

In my journey and research, I have learned that some of us have a hard time allowing our hearts to be open and feel love. We may have walled ourselves off to protect ourselves from being overrun or overwhelmed by others, which may have happened in the recent or distant past by parents, siblings, strangers, or lovers. Some of us may now actually avoid love. When potential love partners pursue them they may detach, disconnect, and disappear emotionally. They are unable to connect, relate, and commit. The mind, based on past experience of being used or abused and unconscious memories, can prevent people from being loving, warm, kind, and sweet. Even in the present, in the face of a wonderful prospective suitor, your past can be a pervasive influence holding you back from love.

Others of us, who were physically or emotionally abandoned, neglected, or left alone a lot, may seek love from the "love-avoider" type of person. They become part of a dance in which the "love-seeker" is attracted to and loves the "love-avoider" in an unconscious attempt to fix the childhood of denied or unfelt love. Yet, as the "love-seeker" gets close, the "love-avoider" retreats, and the past plays out again.

The only way out of this repetitive cycle is for both the "love seeker" and the "love avoider" to become conscious of their patterns and to "cease and desist" pursuing and running away until awareness, *self-love,* and *self-care* skills are gained. Then the "love-seeker" will be able to provide love to himself or herself, and the "love-avoider" will strengthen his or her capacity to feel love, not become overwhelmed by the feeling of love, and able to set appropriate boundaries and express feelings and needs.

Recovery of love through this individual healing of the heart has to take place before conscious, loving partnerships and loving families can take their place worldwide on a large scale.

7 Keys to Love will provide opportunities for healing the heart through a look at the *transformational love process* and the *content of seven dimensions of love,* giving each of us new expressions through which we can pour out our love to reach others and affect the world. Our planet needs love. If we don't heal our hearts and express our love for the planet, we will increasingly experience suffering in the environment and in humanity. We are in an *Age of Global Transformation.* All our ways of doing business will need to change.

After over thirty years of working in community and interna-

THE TRANSFORMATIONAL LOVE PROCESS

 1

Overwhelmed
or abused

Hurt, abandoned,
or love-denied

Fearful

Closed hearted

 2

Powerful mind

Calculating, organized,
efficient, effective . . .

Ego driven,
self-protection

Can become driven
by desire for material
success, selfish, closed-
hearted, cold-hearted
and avoiding love

Narcissistic love

 3

Conscious—
Mindful

Heart healing

Healthy self-love

Compassion

Forgiveness

Loving-kindness

Joy

Warmth

Sweetness

 4

Seeking love

 5

Healing and
overcoming denied
or rejected love

 6

Being love
each day
Praising others

7

Global—Universal Love and Unconditional Love

tional development in the arts, entertainment, health and human services, peace, and the environment with business leaders, educators, social workers, community developers, environmentalists, peacemakers, and artists, I realized that before we can really heal the environment we need to heal humanity's broken heart and transform our economic system, which is harming nature. Our present economic system is based on fear and consumption to fill up our physical, emotional, intellectual, spiritual, social, and cultural emptiness. It creates a competitive, loveless existence—no matter how many toys we acquire and collect.

Hell or Heaven on Earth

You may have heard the story about the people eating in hell, starving because they only had ridiculously huge utensils to feed themselves and it was very cumbersome to eat . . . while the people in heaven were using the very same utensils, but were feeding each other across the table. In the same way, we need a new global economic system based on collaboration and caring for each other and the earth—one that is synergic with nature and embraces higher human potential and love. Before we can fully invent this new kind of economic system we need to heal ourselves first, and then each other.

One thing we can do in the present is to *lovingly enjoy today immensely,* and share that love and joy where we are and in our e-mails. In this way we may help to heal ourselves and humanity's heart a little bit . . . and then the world.

Even if we find ourselves unloved by another, it is possible to feel daily self-love and express it in the seven dimensions of love that will be explored in the book. This loving outlook will give readers the energy and confidence to deal with the difficult things they need to handle. Even in the face of disappointment and defeat, self-love and expressions of love can create hopeful possibilities as we take care of ourselves, and we will be able to take action each day to deal with whatever happens in our lives. We will feel love—no matter what, no matter where, no matter whom we are with.

We can choose to believe in a higher consciousness of love to help us deal with life, enjoy life, and save the planet. May your God, by any name, be a source of love for you.

Each of us needs to firmly believe in our self, and be aware that we each have some gift we can bring to the world. The t-shirt slogan "Hugs Not Drugs" reminds us of the power of love. Why do we do drugs and other destructive behaviors? Because we don't love ourselves. "Love is all we need," sang John Lennon, meaning transformational love will enable you to be loved every day, share love with others, and transform the world with your love.

7 Keys to Love will bring incredible benefits to your life each day. You will learn to express seven facets of love: self-love; physical love; emotional love with friends, family, and others; love for parents and elders; love for ideas and improving the community and society; love for the creative arts and the creative process involved in hobbies; and love for nature, the creation, and the Creator, however you think of it—as God, Great Spirit, Holy Spirit, Higher Power, or Source of the universe. These *seven keys to love* will make you happier than you can imagine. Here is a sample of expressions of love:

> *There are many paths to enlightenment.*
> *Be sure to take the one with a heart.*
> —Lao Tzu

> *Look at every path closely and deliberately,*
> *then ask ourselves this crucial question:*
> *does this path have a heart?*
> *If it does, then the path is good.*
> *If it doesn't, it is of no use.*
> —Carlos Castaneda

> *Someday, after we have mastered the winds,*
> *the waves, the tides and gravity,*
> *we shall harness for God the energies of love.*
> *Then, for the second time*
> *in the history of the world, (hu)mankind*
> *will have discovered fire.*
> —Teilhard de Chardin

Love and do what you will.
—St. Augustine

*A coward is incapable of exhibiting love;
it is the prerogative of the brave.*
—Mahatma Gandhi

Love is life. And if you miss love, you miss life.
—Leo Buscaglia

*When the power of love overcomes the love of power
the world will know peace.*
—Jimi Hendricks

*. . . .all your actions and relationships will reflect
the oneness with all life that you sense deep within.
This is love. Laws, commandments, rules and
regulations are necessary for those who are cut off
from who they are, the Truth within . . .*
—Eckhart Tolle, *A New Earth,
Awakening to Your Life's Purpose*

WORLD LOVE COACH

The *7 Keys to Love* book, workshop, and online learning community will foster healthy experiences and expressions of love: physical, emotional, intellectual, cultural, social, and spiritual, and love for nature.

You may have noticed some of the *7 Painful Processes* in partnerships and couples that can lead to communication breakdowns and the relationship essentially going out of existence. We will practice the *7 Transformational Processes* to build relationships and fully enjoy life with each other.

7 Painful Processes	**7 Transformational Processes**
1. Unforgiving	1. Forgiveness and compassion
2. Judgmental	2. Nonjudgmental
3. Uncommitted to the relationship	3. Commitment to the relationship
4. Uncommunicative	4. Compassionate communication
5. Inflexible and unwilling to change and try again	5. Flexibility and willingness to change and try again
6. Not participating in problem solving	6. Full participation in creative problem solving
7. Inability to be warm, loving, and passionate	7. Ability to be warm, loving, and passionate

I encourage men and women to be warm. Many have become cold because they had unloving relationships in the past. The following is the scale of the *7 Positions of Warmth:*

7 Positions of Warmth

1. Hateful	4. Cool	6. Warming up
2. Hurtful	5. Thawing out	7. Being warm
3. Cold		

Yes . . . you can have a warm and passionate love life!
Believe and it will happen!!!

—Sandy Hinden, World Love Coach :-)

CHAPTER 1

Self-Love

Love is the great miracle cure.
Loving ourselves works miracles in our lives.
—LOUISE L. HAY

When love brings conflict, failure, rejection, disappointment, and humiliation . . . yuk . . . who wants it? . . . The heck with love! . . . Love can hurt us . . . and hurt our self-esteem. So why try again?

A woman told me about a man she met online. She went to meet him in a far away place . . . they had a nice time . . . but when she came back home she realized he wasn't the one. She carefully told him she did not want an "exclusive" relationship.

The man had decided to move back to his home state, which was where she lived, and when he arrived, they met again because she was so nice and he was so interested in her. They enjoyed each other again, but she continued to let him know that although they could remain life-long friends, she wanted to go out with others.

She e-mailed me and said she felt terrible letting him down, and asked if I had any advice for her. I wrote back with this . . . .

She wrote:

I'm getting the sense that he is grieving from this disconnect, and I feel terrible . . . any advice dr?

I wrote:

We each create our own reality each day . . . so until he gets that you are not the right person for him, he will continue to grieve the loss . . .

He needs to clearly see he would not be good with you . . . because you don't feel what he would like you to feel about him . . .

He needs to love himself the way he would like you to love him . . . that is our daily work before our beloved shows up . . .

How's that?

She wrote:

I understand and know this, but it's wonderful the way you worded it. My appreciation . . .

How did I know so clearly what he needed to do with himself and her? It came from many years of working on self-love, and learning that unless we deeply love ourselves, we may attract and attach ourselves to someone who doesn't really "get us" and really love us deeply. We may settle for "crumbs of love," mistake sex for love, or sell out for money or power and the apparent freedom they can buy us.

It was also easy for me to put it into words because she had told me about him when I first began communicating with her online, two months before, exploring possibilities between us. After a month of wonderful phone calls and fun text messages, she told me she was not interested in an exclusive relationship with me either.

So, I had worked through my pain with her a month before.

Then there was a month of silence between us . . . and then I received an e-mail notice from her. I was one of many the e-mail was addressed to, telling us that she had a new e-mail address . . . hmmm . . .

I e-mailed her with an update of what I was up to, and she sent me her update that she had essentially ended the romantic possibility of a relationship with the other fellow . . . and she asked for my advice.

I felt for the guy because I felt the same way about her. She is an attractive, spiritual, hardworking, good-hearted woman, and after she rebuffed me, I had to lick my wounds and return to self-love. I had to get over grieving her loss and move on.

From many years of personal work, I knew that we each create our own reality each day, through our thoughts, attitudes, and actions. I needed to clearly be aware and accept that she was not the right woman for me, and would not be good for me, because she didn't feel what I would like her to feel for me. She didn't have the same enthusiasm for me as I had for her . . . nor enthusiasm for the possibilities we could create together by helping each other create each other's dreams . . . nor enthusiasm for our love for each other.

I had realized, in my month apart from her, and my twenty years of self-work, that I needed to love myself the way I wanted her to love me . . . that is my daily work before my beloved shows up.

I MARRY MYSELF FIRST

It must be wonderful to grow up in a high-nurturance family. Unfortunately many of us did not experience high-nurturance families, schools, and communities, so we need to re-parent, love, and nurture ourselves. John Bradshaw wrote that 95% of us grew up in dysfunctional families.

Most of us want someone to love, honor, and cherish us. We

want to be with our beloved. Whether we are in a marriage or are single, we want to feel deeply appreciated and loved.

Through the years, I have learned to see three aspects of the Beloved.

1. **God the Beloved:** The Beloved-as-God . . . we will explore more about this in the chapter on spiritual-universal love, about love for the Source of the universe, the Creator, Creation, Holy Spirit, Great Spirit, Higher Power, God . . . whatever you call the wonderful mystery that created the universe.

2. **My Partner the Beloved:** The second aspect of the Beloved is seeing your partner as the beloved. In India people say namaste. The divinity within me salutes the divinity in you. We will explore this in the chapters on emotional love and again in spiritual-universal love.

3. **The Beloved Within:** The third aspect of the Beloved is seeing your self as a spark of divine loving-light, or as made in the image and likeness of God, or as being a practice and expression of the higher-self qualities of serenity, courage, wisdom, love, compassion, forgiveness, kindness, devotion, goodwill, determination, patience, persistence, and conflict resolution to harmony. We can acquire and practice these higher qualities in our Life as a Creative Journey and will look at them in chapter on spiritual-universal love.

The beginning of self-love came for me when I asked a therapist, "How do you develop self-love?" She said, "Forget about self-love. Develop self-care . . . learn to take really good care of yourself."

Many of us, to get over loneliness or to recover from relationships that didn't work out, have to learn how to get over hurt, rejection, low self-image, low self-esteem, comparing ourselves to others, a sense of nagging inferiority, inadequacy, or feeling not being good enough, not having enough, or doing well enough. We drive ourselves crazy seeking outer love, while we forgot how to or never learn how to fully appreciate ourselves to begin with. We never learned how to take good care of ourselves or just forget to take good care of our body, emotions, mind, and spirit with healthy food, water, rest, clothing, shelter, work, finances, play, and relationships.

Love Your Shadows

There is that part of ourselves that feels ugly, deformed, unacceptable. That part, above all, we must learn to cherish, embrace, and call by name.

—MACRINA WIEDERKEHR

Before you can fully love yourself you need to understand the parts of yourself that you define as "good" and "bad." The characteristics that you reject need to be accepted and loved. You need to honor them or they will continue to assert themselves by doing whatever they can to get your attention. What parts of yourself do you reject? Take some time to see the parts of yourself you do not love. Be completely open and honest about each one. What was the wound? What need was operating that gave rise to its condition? When you accept, appreciate, love, and have compassion for your wounded, unaccepted parts and needs, they will heal.

. . .self-contempt never inspires lasting change.

—JANE R. HIRSCHMANN AND CAROL H. MUNTER

The first step toward change is acceptance.
Once you accept yourself, you open the door to change.
That's all you have to do.
Change is not something you do, it's something you allow.

—WILL GARCIA

WHAT ASPECTS OF YOURSELF DO YOU REJECT?	WITH DEEP COMPASSION, I ACCEPT AND LOVE MY . . .
1.	
2.	
3.	

SELF-VALUING, SELF-APPRECIATION

I have a friend, Faridi McFree, an interfaith minister, artist, and author. In 1982 she published book called *CELEBRATE YOU! Self-Healing Through Art and Affirmations.* Faridi is an amazing woman. She was one of the pioneers in the creative human potential movement and founded the Studio of the Healing Hearts. To celebrate life and yourself, to realize that *life is a gift* and you are a gift fosters a sense of loving your self, loving others, loving your life and loving Life itself . . . truly amazing. We are living life on what could be the most beautiful planet in the universe and rarely glimpse that. Let's repeat that . . .

> *Let us appreciate*
> *that we are living life*
> *on what could be the*
> *most beautiful planet*
> *in the universe . . .*

Appreciation is the key to enjoying life in all it splendors . . . appreciation of nature, art and music appreciation, appreciation for good books and theater, appreciation for people, and appreciation for yourself. In *The Secret* by Rhonda Byrne, the *inner secret* of the Law of Attraction is to *feel* grateful and happy each day, because that feeling-energy sets up a vibrational energy that lets other know *you are safe and fun to be with.* That allows them to safely offer you opportunities.

So, self-happiness, self-appreciation, valuing yourself, others, and life, opens the door to inner and outer abundance. The more value you place on yourself and others, the more others will value you. The more you appreciate them and yourself, the more they will show their appreciation for you. Self-love starts with valuing yourself and appreciation of yourself. It starts a chain reaction of inner appreciation leading to outer success.

SELF-FORGIVENESS, SELF-COMPASSION

After a while, on life's journey, you discover you have a lesser-self and a better-self. A lower-self and a higher-self.

Sometimes you may "fall off the wagon," or veer off "the path," "the way," and walk the low road.

At other times you are "working the program." You are on the path each day and occasionally have a breakthrough to a higher and farther dimension. You take the high road to the mountain-top, where you can see forever. Then you return from the mountaintop and come back to act on your higher values. By engaging in actions and activities to create a better life based on your higher values, your self-esteem goes up. You know exactly when you are doing that.

To have a foundation of loving yourself, you need to be devoted to yourself, even when you have a setback and veer off the path and your shortcomings—character defects, faults, weaknesses, bad habits, less well-developed character traits, or over-developed strong traits—resurface during the trials and tribulations of life.

This is when your vices kick-in to *numb the pain* of daily life, and compulsive-addictive behaviors reappear. When you say amazingly foolish or hurtful words. When your "story" takes over again. When your overused strong suits make a mess trying to overpower, fix, change, or control others. When you become judgmental, ego-driven, selfish, self-seeking or narcissistic. When you become inauthentic, lazy, frightened, angry, nasty, and more.

When any of these happen, you need to create a clearing in your life. Create a sacred space for your self to heal once again. Create a space to become empty again, so you can return to the Zen of *Beginners Mind.*

Return to self-forgiveness and compassion for yourself, the salve of self-love. This helps you establish that *no matter what happens or does not happen, your love for yourself will never be blotted out by anyone or anything big or small, by any situation or circumstance in life.*

SELF-RESPECT, SELF-ESTEEM

What is your opinion of yourself? What are you like when you are alone? Do you treat yourself kindly? Are you harsh with yourself? Are you judgmental with yourself? Do you have a critical inner-voice that is picky, fussy, or perfectionist, envious of others, a master at self putdowns? If so, this inner-voice, your self-talk, will damage your self-concept and self-esteem.

Changing your harsh inner-voice to a supportive, empowering inner-voice is possible. I know this because I have done it. I used to have an introjected inner-voice that I picked up from my grandmother when I was a child. She was a wonderful grandmother, but she was critical and judgmental of others. So, I learned her way of thinking and communicating and it became my inner-voice.

Where did the harsh inner-voice in your head come from—a parent, grandparent, older sibling, teacher, religious leader, a tough coach? It's time to let it go and start practicing kinder and gentler phrases. Instead of punishing yourself with a critical parent voice, guide yourself to doing esteemable acts with guidance from your higher-self, nurturing parent, higher power, Great Spirit or whatever you call the still, quiet, patient, wise inner-voice. Listen quietly and you will hear it. It will guide you to doing things that will be in your best interest and truly in the best interest of others. Keep doing *the next best thing* to do in your life.

> *We do good*
> *because it frees the heart.*
> *It opens us to a wellspring of happiness.*
> —SHARON SALZBERG

Esteemable acts, based on your values, are the actions that we are proud of. The more we do them, the better we feel. Be aware of what you do that makes you feel guilty and shameful and avoid these actions. Recoil from them, don't do them as much as possible. That includes engaging in disempowering conversations, being overbearing, and hurting other's feelings while trying to get what you want, wasting your time, overspending, bad habits, and addictions.

You are the architect of your life . . . design a blueprint and follow it. You are the director of your new life-script. You are the pilot of the plane of your life . . . stay on course, keep in mind where you want to go and where you are heading, get feedback and make course corrections. Keep taking constructive actions to meet your most important priorities and your self-respect and self-esteem and will skyrocket.

> *Be who you need to be*
> *to be consistent with*
> *what you are trying to create.*

SELF-NURTURING, SELF-COMFORTING, SELF-SOOTHING

Self-love can grow when you form a union with yourself and you nourish it. That relationship with yourself will strengthen a beloved partnership with yourself that will endure all the days of your life. When difficult situations occur, when your love is denied or thwarted, stonewalled or discarded, you will comfort yourself and apply self-soothing.

When you feel emotional pain or irritation, it is important to calm and relax your body, gently talk with yourself, light a candle or some incense, put on some soothing music. Be your own best friend. Create your home as your soothing sanctuary and practice self-nurturing, comforting, and soothing skills.

SELF-SWEETNESS, DAILY SELF-CARE

Self-kindness heals the daily wrath of foolish men and women. People and life can be a challenge. Self-sweetness can be a blessing.

Self-sweetness is the further dimension of human development. This skill will be an amazing breakthrough for you.

Self-Sweetness Skills

- Whisper the word *sweetheart*. Hear it ring . . . say it again, gently, lovingly.
- Feel your heart relax. *Sweetheart* . . .
- Feel the appreciation in your heart that you are speaking to it sweetly.
- Call yourself *sweetheart*.
- Speak to yourself as you want your beloved to speak to you.
- Call yourself *dear, honey, darling*.

Self-Nurturing, Comforting, and Soothing Skills

- Stop self-harming thoughts and actions. Be patient, understanding, and kind with yourself.

- Stop acting out to get revenge or get attention. Be forgiving of others, in your past and in the present.

- Stop seeking instant gratification. Be accepting of a delay in gratification or the lack of gratification in a situation.

- Stop having expectations of others and making yourself right and the other person wrong. Be accepting of people—who they are and who they're not.

- Stop trying to control what you feel or do not feel, or trying to control or manipulate others. Be accepting of what you feel or don't feel. Take care of yourself and your own business.

- Stop punishing those in your life for the mistakes and wrongdoings of people in your past. Be present and take action to create the life you want in the present.

- Stop devaluing and being critical of yourself and others. Be appreciative of and value yourself and others.

- Stop being distrustful of yourself and others. Be understanding of how and what you feel and need.

- Stop demanding that others fulfill your needs. Give space to others and take space to be alone with your self. Fulfill your own needs. Give and take. Surrender control and go with the flow.

- Stop being inauthentic and hiding your feelings and needs. Be authentic and tell the truth to yourself. When you are with trustworthy people, share what is real for you with them. Share your feelings and needs. Make requests, not demands.

- Stop being harsh with yourself if you backslide or make a mistake. Be gentle with yourself if you backslide or make a mistake.

See how wonderful it feels. Speak to yourself patiently, with understanding, especially in times of sorrow and tribulation. This will create courage and confidence in you because you are there to back yourself up. You are re-parenting yourself and marrying yourself.

It is my recommendation that you *love, honor,* and *cherish* yourself with kindness and sweetness. I suggest that you marry yourself, in sacred ceremony, where you agree *to love, honor,* and *cherish* yourself, *till death do you part* from this life.

Love has no other desire but to fulfill itself.
To wake at dawn with a winged heart and give thanks
to another day of loving;
To rest at the noon hour and meditate love's ecstasy;
To return home eventide with gratitude;
And then sleep with a prayer for the beloved in your heart
and a song of praise upon your lips.

—KAHLIL GIBRAN

Take good care of yourself each day. Eat healthy food. Drink enough water or healthy beverages. Walk or exercise regularly. Do yoga or Tai Chi. Meditate. Get enough rest. All men and women need to nurture and take good care of themselves.

Be empowering to yourself and others. Do what you love to do. Follow your bliss, healthy passions, and healthy pleasures. Laugh, sing, dance, play, draw, and write. Be fully expressive and fully creative. Love yourself, love yourself, love yourself sweetly . . . and live a life you love!

FROM NARCISSISM TO SELF-LOVE

Self-love is not narcissism. It is a process to get to self-love by expanding our conscious awareness and taming our ego, which is there to differentiate the self from the herd and to protect the self. Unfortunately, the ego can become dysfunctional, self-centered, selfish, and self-serving, trapped in its own story and in self-seeking for power and control.

The way out of the *trap of the ego* is to keep expanding your consciousness and love for yourself, by letting-go and giving up all that you don't need to have a healthy, happy, love-filled life.

1. Primary Experience

- Low nurturance in the family, school, and community
- In some cases neglect, abuse, or abandonment

2. Primary Consciousness

- Low self-love and self-esteem
- Distorted thinking
- Distrust

3. Primary Expressions

- Self-protection, self-centeredness, selfishness
- Seeking power and control over others

4. Expansion of Consciousness

- Awareness of old patterns of thinking and behavior
- Mindfulness of the present
- Willingness to change

5. True Self-Love

- Compassion, forgiveness, self-comforting, and self-sweetness
- High self-esteem and self-love
- Full creative expression
- Mutual appreciation and creative collaboration

When we expand our consciousness, we become aware of how toxic certain thinking, habits, behaviors, activities, expressions, people, relationships, situations, and patterns are. We clearly see they are not healthy for us and not in our best interest.

It is part of the spiritual process
to disconnect from that which is unhealthy
and connect with what is healthy and supportive
of further growth and conscious expansion.

Self-love is essential for a wonderful life based on our conscious character development, remaking our self to be our fuller self, and living a life of higher power and higher purpose. Living a life you are truly in love with, because you truly love yourself.

FROM TOUGH LOVE TO SELF-LOVE

One of the things I do to help the world is assist organizations with planning, public relations, marketing, and fundraising. I visited a friend of mine, Suzanne Riordan, in Santa Barbara to help her with her new organization, Families ACT, Families Advocating for Compassionate Treatment.

The purpose of the organization is to help young people with the dual diagnosis of bipolar (high-low, happy-sad) thinking and feeling and drug addiction. Suzanne started the organization because a number of young people died of drug overdoses in Santa Barbara around the same time, including her wonderful twenty-five-year-old son Ian, because there are no effective treatment programs for the dually diagnosed. This is a process of mental illness that leads to alcohol and drug addiction, jail, and further harm. She states on the Families ACT webpage (www.familiesact.org):

Over 70 people in Santa Barbara county died of drug overdose or suicide in 2006. Santa Barbarans with mental illness and addiction are often jailed when treatment is what is needed. Yet our jail is critically overcrowded. In Santa Barbara county, in order to get an emergency mental health assessment for a family member, you cannot call for a mental health assessment team, but must call the police! We do not have beds available in a locked medical psychiatric ward in our county. Our dually diagnosed who need this are on the streets, housed in jail, or shipped to other counties. One of the two largest housing facilities for our mentally ill nationwide is the Los Angeles County Jail. In 1998 co-occurring substance use disorders and mental health conditions affected up to 8 million individuals in the U.S. each year. Almost all substance abusers and addicts need treatment to become clean and sober. The vast majority of them will not do it on their own. Effective treatment is more than medication. The longer someone remains in treatment, the more successful he or she generally is in maintaining sobriety. Most studies have found that one year is the minimum effective duration. The United States has the highest prison population rate in the world. In 2004, 6.9 million adults, or one out of every 32 Americans was incarcerated or on probation or parole. One in four Americans has a family member who is struggling with addiction. In 2005, there were 23.2 million Americans who needed treatment for their illicit drug or alcohol abuse problems, yet only about 10% received the treatment they needed.

On my trip to Santa Barbara and since then, I found out that many programs for teens and young adults in trouble are based on tough love.

Affirmations for Self-Love

- I value my being and life as the sun and stars shine . . .

- I appreciate my heart, my dreams, and my efforts . . .

- I forgive myself, others, and life for all that did not go as I wished . . .

- I have compassion for my own and other's mistakes . . . and I learn from them . . .

- I respect others and myself; we are all incredibly worthy because we have the amazing gift of life within us . . .

- I have high-esteem and do what gently allows dignity within me to grow day by day . . .

- I nurture my hopes, dreams, wishes, goals, plans, and daily efforts to create a wonderful life . . .

- I gently notice if conflict, failure, rejection, disappointment, humiliation, frustration, fear, hurt, or pain come my way and activate anger in me . . .

- I quickly let go of anger, resentment, being right, and making others wrong . . .

- I return to being calm, relaxed, and patient . . .

- I refocus on what I can do that is in my best interest and the interest if others . . .

- I deeply soothe and comfort myself with people and life . . . each day . . .

- I am sweet, kind, and gentle with myself each day . . .

- I take good care of myself each day . . .

- I love, honor, and cherish myself . . .

CHAPTER 2

Emotional Love

Emotional love comes in many flavors. It happens in our love for family, friends, coworkers, caregivers who help us, our pets. An emotional energy of love passes from us to to all those we care about most through our presence and our expressions of compassion and concern—it nourishes them, heals them, and makes them grow.

We are most human when we love others and they love us. Life can be so difficult with economic upsets and environmental challenges, yet with love—when we care about others and they care about us—the shocks of life are made easier. When we are kind and gentle to the people we care about we too feel nourished. It is so important to develop the nurturing inner voice within and to use it with others and ourselves each day.

	NEGATIVE	POSITIVE
Thoughts	Critical, judgmental	Trust, appreciation
Feelings	Anger, envy, jealousy, resentment	Love
Words	Undermining, put-downs, beating up on ourselves and others	Empowering ourselves and others, constructive feedback
Behaviors, Actions	Competitive and destructive	Creative collaboration

Emotional love is based on certain thoughts, which produce certain feelings, words and actions.

Emotions—e-motions—are feelings that seem to generate themselves inside us as a response to what is going on in our outer world and our own thinking.

We have basic emotions, or feelings, of being sad, scared, mad, or glad, and all of their variations. If we pay attention to them, and interpret the feeling by putting a word on it, we are naming the feeling and the message inside the feeling. These messages can tell us what is going on inside us and around us. Having "emotional intelligence" includes emotional-feeling awareness, feeling interpretation, and naming the feeling. In a sense, you can take your emotional temperature, from being frozen to cold, cool, lukewarm, warm, hot, to boiling over. On the next page are variations of sad, scared, mad, and glad.

THE POWER OF LOVING WORDS

Words work. They either create love or diminish it. It is important to share positive, supportive, kind, loving words with those you love. Yet we are brought up with judgmental criticism, cynicism and sarcasm all around us. The following will help you reclaim and develop the power of words to create love in your life through joy and praise, encouragement and warmth.

If you use harsh, judgmental, critical words
you will not be able to feel love in your life.

Word Substitution

Where did the harsh, critical, judgmental words in our head come from? In Chapter One we learned that they come from the harsh, critical, judgmental words of the people and media that we grew up with.

SAD	SCARED	MAD
Betrayed	Anxious	Agitated
Chronically tired	Doubtful	Arrogant
Depressed	Fearful	Hostile
Disappointed	Worried	Rebellious
Withdrawn		Snotty

GLAD

ENTHUSIASTIC

Absorbed	Ecstatic	Giddy	Rejuvenated
Alert	Elated	Happy	Renewed
Amazed	Enchanted	Interested	Rested
Animated	Energetic	Inspired	Restored
Ardent	Engaged	Intrigued	Revived
Aroused	Engrossed	Invigorated	Spellbound
Astonished	Enlivened	Involved	Stimulated
Awed	Enthralled	Joyful	Surprised
Blissful	Entranced	Lively	Thrilled
Curious	Excited	Passionate	Tickled
Creative	Exhilarated	Radiant	Vibrant
Dazzled	Exuberant	Rapturous	Wonder
Eager	Fascinated	Refreshed	

EMPOWERED

Appreciative	Centered	Flexible	Proud
Bold	Clear headed	Moved	Safe
Brave	Confident	Open	Secure
Buoyant	Courageous	Optimistic	Thankful
Calm	Encouraged	Positive	Touched

LOVING

Affectionate	Fulfilled	Open hearted	Serene
Amused	Glad	Optimistic	Sweet
Comfortable	Grateful	Peaceful	Sympathetic
Compassionate	Happy	Pleased	Tender
Content	Hopeful	Quiet	Tranquil
Delighted	Joyful	Relaxed	Trusting
Expectant	Jubilant	Relieved	Warm
Friendly	Mellow	Satisfied	

How can we get rid of the harsh, critical, judgmental words in our head? It can take time to acquire and use a new vocabulary of peacefulness, compassion, forgiveness, appreciation, support, kindness, and love. The words we use create a feeling state inside us. Changing our vocabulary is not easy for many of us. We have to just stop using harsh, judgmental words when we hear them in our head. We need to catch ourselves when we say them to others and stop and switch to more positive constructive, solution-focused, empowering words. By changing the words we use in the world, the world will change.

Words create our world.

Transactional Analysis

Years ago, I learned an interpersonal relations model that helped me understand the different voices we can hear in our head and from others. It was called Transactional Analysis (TA). Whenever I show people the model, they always say I should write a book about it. There have been books written about TA in the past. *I'm OK - You're OK* was one of them. Here is the basic model of TA, and then a more advance model I learned in a workshop.

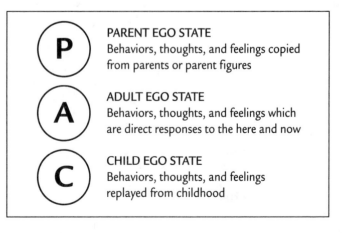

P

PARENT EGO STATE
Behaviors, thoughts, and feelings copied from parents or parent figures

A

ADULT EGO STATE
Behaviors, thoughts, and feelings which are direct responses to the here and now

C

CHILD EGO STATE
Behaviors, thoughts, and feelings replayed from childhood

The diagram at right shows what it looks like when two people have a verbal transaction.

When we take a closer look at what makes up various parental and child states and statements it looks like the diagram below.

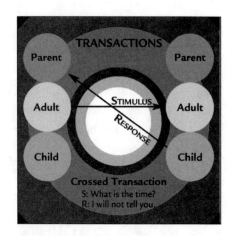

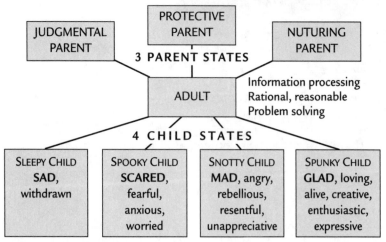

The Nurturing Parent and the Judgmental Parent

As adults, our expressions of love come from our nurturing parent state, in which we use caring, compassionate, cooperative, collaborative, comforting, soothing, forgiving, sweet, sharing, and kind words. Yet, we are living in a competitive world where harshness and selfishness are commonplace in the media, down mean streets, in bitter divorces, though schoolyard bullies. Ultimately, the disempowering expressions from the judgmental parental state can create terrorist acts and result in global war.

Mass Judgmental Thinking

The powerful judgmental mind in our world seems to be engendering a new kind of "mass mental illness," made up of people ranging from those who are less functional to highly functional people who use cynicism and sarcasm in their daily endeavors. These fall into three categories, each requiring a different "cure:"

The Three Mass Mental Illnesses of Society

• Excess individualism, egotism, narcissism, self-absorption, self-importance, status hunger, hyper-competition

• Power hunger, aggressive-sarcastic-cynical words, violence

• Greed, possessiveness, selfishness, materialism

Their Cure

• Self-healing; respect, appreciation, and love for self and others; empathy, cooperation, love

• Calmness, power with others, mutual empowerment

• Sharing, generosity, community, community development aligned with nature

Where there is charity and wisdom,
there is neither fear nor ignorance.

Where there is patience and humility,
there is neither anger nor annoyance.

Where there is love and joy,
there is neither greed nor selfishness.

Where there is peace and meditation,
there is neither anxiety nor doubt.

—PARAPHRASED FROM ST. FRANCIS OF ASSISI

A World of Love, Without War

How can the *terrorist mindset* of judgmental bitterness be pre-vented and replaced with love? The terrorist mindset is being fed by lack of education and a lively weapons and war business—harshness with a motive and a profitable reward. Sometimes we may feel hopeless about creating a transformed world. I have learned that the way out of terribly difficult situations is though what we call transcendent solutions. *Loving our enemy* is one such solution. While working on the US Department of Peace Campaign I connected with Ret. Air Force Captain and Department of Defense Comptroller Edward Winchester, founder of the Pentagon Meditation Club. As a volunteer for the Club, I created a Transformation Project and discovered this quote:

> "Men since the beginning of time have sought peace . . . Military alliances, balances of power, leagues of nations, all in turn have failed, leaving the only path to be by way of the crucible of war . . . We have had our last chance. If we do not now devise some greater and more equitable system, Armageddon will be at our door. The problem is basically theological and involves a spiritual recrudescence (transformation) and improvement of human character that will synchronize with our almost matchless advances in science, art, literature, and all material and cultural developments of the past two thousand years. It must be of the spirit if we are to save the flesh."
>
> —General Douglas MacArthur

To learn to love our enemy, here is another idea . . .

We can foster the creation of a *Center for Meditation, Communication, and Mediation* in each country of the world. These Centers can be supported by an *International Association of Centers for Meditation, Communication, and Mediation*.

Nonviolent (Compassionate) Communication

In such centers, Transactional Analysis can be taught along with *Nonviolent (Compassionate) Communication (NVC)*, which was developed to help people through a simple four-step compassionate communication process. NVC is a practical, concrete set of skills for making connections of compassionate giving and receiving based in a consciousness of interdependence and power with others. These skills include:

1. **Observing:** Differentiating observation from evaluation, being able to carefully observe what is happening free of evaluation, and being able to specify behaviors and conditions that are affecting us;

2. **Feelings:** Differentiating feeling from thinking, being able to identify and express internal feeling states in a way that does not imply judgment, criticism, blame and/or punishment;

3. **Values/Needs:** Connecting with the universal human values and needs (for example, sustenance, trust, understanding) in us that are being met or not met in relation to what is happening and how we are feeling; understanding our needs.

4. **Requests:** Requesting what we would like in a way that clearly and specifically states what we do want rather than what we don't want, and that truly is a request and not a demand (for example, attempting to motivate, however subtly, out of fear, guilt, shame, obligation, and so on rather than out of willingness and compassionate giving).

See **www.cnvc.org.**

Helping Bullies, Terrorists, and the Anti-Social Learn to Love

So many people in the world do not seem ready, willing, or able to love. Bullies, terrorists, and the antisocial were abused, neglected, or abandoned children who were not shown how to be compassionate, reasonable, and respectful of others. They began to hang out with the wrong crowd or became loners. They need help but rarely get it, because they can be stubborn and difficult to approach.

Bullies come from homes where there was little warmth and parental attention. Discipline may have taken the form of using physical punishment, harsh emotional outbursts or constant criticism. Conversations were harsh, judgmental, or nonexistent. Helping bullies learn *empathy* and guiding them so they can meet their needs for *empowerment in a constructive* way and have *loving relationships* would go a long way to improve the world. It is important to help bullies and the antisocial learn to obtain their goals without hurting others, learn to trust trustworthy people, and to delay gratification and form relationships with helping adults.

- Do you know any bullies?

- How do you feel about them?

- Would you be willing to help them learn to have constructive conversation?

- You can begin by practicing NVC, Nonviolent (Compassionate) Communication, and then trying to have constructive conversations with them and even teaching them NVC.

Bullies may have been exposed to a lot of violence on television, in movies, and in video games that glorify violence as a means of problem solving. They often lack empathy and never consider the feelings of their victims and consider teasing and name-calling to be "all in fun." Help them discuss their feelings and the feelings of others. They tend to focus on negative traits and derive much of their humor from jokes about the shortcomings of others. Talk about what is right and good in others, what you admire and appreciate about others. When their strengths are refocused, bullies can make great heroes and defenders. Praise them when they stick up for others and do constructive acts.

In the film *Batman: The Dark Knight,* the Joker had a line ". . . and some people just want to watch the world burn." After I heard that, I began interviewing malicious people to understand their psyche.

There is a gigantic world industry based on creating pain for others (war, weapons trade, genocide as seen in Darfur, media, the Goth darkness teen style, violent screaming rock, violent video games).

I looked up the word *malice* and found:

mal•ice : FUNCTION: noun; ETYMOLOGY: Middle English, from Anglo-French, from Latin malitia, from malus bad; DATE: 14th century

1 : desire to cause pain, injury, or distress to another

2 : intent to commit an unlawful act or cause harm without legal justification or excuse

SYNONYMS: malice, malevolence, ill will, spite, malignity, spleen, grudge mean the desire to see another experience pain, injury, or distress.

- malice implies a deep-seated often unexplainable desire to see another suffer "felt no malice toward their former enemies"
- malevolence suggests a bitter persistent hatred that is likely to be expressed in malicious conduct "a look of dark malevolence"
- ill will implies a feeling of antipathy of limited duration "ill will provoked by a careless remark"
- spite implies petty feelings of envy and resentment that are often expressed in small harassments "petty insults inspired by spite"
- malignity implies deep passion and relentlessness "a life consumed by motiveless malignity"
- spleen suggests the wrathful release of latent spite or persistent malice "venting his spleen against politicians"
- grudge implies a harbored feeling of resentment or ill will that seeks satisfaction "never one to harbor a grudge"

—Merriam-Webster Online (www.merriam-webster.com)

I think the root of malice is caused when children are young; many felt *unwanted, unappreciated, and unloved* by parents and people around them. They grew up with bitterness around them and it is still in them. The bitterness can be healed and released, but they hold-carry grudges and don't want to let it go. They may have a value-culture-feeling of revenge that can be perpetuated in the next generation, which fosters bitterness, hatred, abuse, or and violence in cycles of revenge for generation after generation.

Are you
ready (at the right time in your life and level of maturity),
willing (have the desire to open your heart to caring
and sharing)
and able (have the communication and sharing skills)
to love?

I want, appreciate, and love myself . . .
I am ready to love another . . .

Emotional Readiness for Love

If you grew up with conscious, wise, loving parents, you were very lucky. Many people grew up feeling neglected, rejected, abandoned, or abused, and hence crave or avoid love. If you felt neglected, rejected, or abandoned, you may seek love desperately. If you felt abused, you may avoid the intimacy of love because you feel your boundaries will be overrun again when people get close.

To be emotionally ready for healthy love, you need to learn to take good care of yourself, nurture your self-esteem, learn to be expressive of your feelings and needs, and make requests for what you want assertively, without being disrespectful and demanding of others.

Being emotionally ready for love can take time to develop.

From Apathy to Empathy—
The Healing Agent of Love

Apathy is an unfeeling, insensitivity to the feeling and suffering of others. Empathy, on the other hand, occurs when the same brain cells in two people light up at the same time. They experience each other's experience. Empathy is essential for caring about each other and loving each other. Empathy only occurs through listening with compassion and willingness to feel and care about another person. If you feel a lot of fear or competition around someone you will not be able to feel empathy with them.

Empathy allows you to try to help someone. It enables you to stand in his or her shoes and see the world from that other person's point of view. People trapped in their own ego can't see the world from another's perspective.

I have a very strong feeling that the opposite of love
is not hate—it's apathy. It's not giving a damn.

—LEO BUSCAGLIA

Fear or Love

It has been said that we experience either LOVE (unity) or FEAR (separation) in our connections with others and the world around us. Both emotions can be used in a positive way when we are able to recognize what we are feeling and react constructively. When fear arises within us, we can use it as an opportunity to bring a certain quality into our life. When we bring higher qualities into the presence of disturbance, the lower energies are transformed. Rather than running away, controlling, suppressing, or resisting fear, we transform it into an incredible experience when we understand what is needed—patience, a conversation about feelings and needs, trust, openness, courage, serenity, kindness, gentleness, compassion, joy, hope, detachment, letting go of the need to fix or change things or control others, minding your own business, nurturing yourself, and so on—in that particular situation. Love heals by transforming the situation into new possibilities.

From Cool to Warm

When we grow up in a judgmental or cool family environment, our hearts may get frozen. It will take a thawing of your heart to go from being icy or cool to being warm and loving.

Before we go through a transformation process that heals our heart we may suffer from poverty of the spirit. We may build an igloo around our heart and our world, creating an environment of coolness and isolation to protect our precious heart, soul, and interior.

After healing our original wound, the ice melts and our world can be filled with warmth, happiness, laughter, and love. We can become committed to being loving and supportive. We can have fear-free communication and relationships, a positive attitude, and the excitement of new doors opening professionally and personally, with warmth and joy.

We can find strength, courage, and love. To love someone deeply can give us strength. Being loved deeply by someone can give us courage. Let us always meet each other with a smile, for a smile is the beginning of love.

THE FIRESTORM AND THE ICEBERG OF EMOTIONS

A simple way to remember that people sometimes don't express their emotions clearly is a model I created called *The Iceberg of Emotions*.

Often, when people are angry they have other feelings going on below the surface. You only experience the expression of anger, while below the surface they have hurt, humiliation, sadness, and or fear.

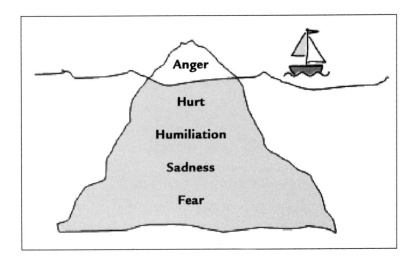

Another metaphor taken from nature is that it may take a gigantic fight, *a firestorm of anger,* for them to realize that expressing anger in an angry way gets them into trouble, while expressing feelings of hurt, humiliation, sadness, and fear has a better outcome for them. They need to learn to share what is below the surface of their anger instead of giving in to the immediate emotion of rage.

Along my life's journey I learned some wise phrases that help when I feel angry . . .

Humility saves me from humiliation.

and

Say what you mean, mean what you say,
but don't say it in a mean way.

If you are an angry person, you can call your family members or others you may have blasted in the past, and apologize. You can create a very kind and loving relationship with them. You will be proud that you can master your anger. Your heart will be calmer and loved ones will be able to get closer to you, even when you are upset.

From the firestorm of anger can grow new seedlings and saplings of understanding and love. Nature has its way . . .

HEALTHY, LOVING RELATIONSHIPS VERSUS LOVE ADDICTION AND LOVE AVOIDANCE

Some of us have a very hard time allowing our hearts to be open and feel love. We have seen that we can wall ourselves off to protect ourselves from being overrun or overwhelmed by others. This may have happened in the recent or distant past by parents, strangers or lovers, but unfortunately we may now actually avoid love as a result. When a potential love partner pursues us, we may detach, disconnect, and disappear emotionally. We do not connect, relate, and commit.

The mind, with its unconscious memories based on your experience of being used or abused in the past, prevents you from being loving, warm, kind, and sweet. Even in the present, in the face of a wonderful prospective suitor, your past can have a pervasive influence, holding you back from love.

Others of us who were physically or emotionally abandoned, neglected, or left alone a lot, may "seek love" from the "love-avoidant" type of person and become part of a dance in which the "love-seeker" loves the "love-avoider" in an attempt to fix the childhood of denied or unfelt love. But as the "love-seeker" gets close, the "love-avoider" retreats, and the past plays out again.

The way out of this repetitive dance cycle is for both the "love-seeker" and "love-avoider" to become conscious of their patterns and to "cease and desist" until awareness, self-love and self-care skills are gained. Then the "love-seeker" will be able to provide love to his or her self and not be so desperate and dependent upon the other person, and the "love-avoider" can strengthen his or her capacity to feel love and not become overwhelmed by the feeling of love, and then will be able to express feelings and needs and set appropriate boundaries.

Love and Sex Addiction

Sex and Love Addiction Anonymous (SLAA) is a twelve-step recovery group for men and women facing issues related to love and sex, including a compulsive need for sex, extreme dependency on one or many people, or a chronic preoccupation with romance, intrigue, or fantasy.

Sometimes love and sex can lead to an obsessive-compulsive pattern, either sexual or emotional, or both. The relationship or sexual activities can become increasingly destructive to career, family, and sense of self-respect.

Sex addiction and love addiction, if left unchecked, always gets worse. SLAA provides a program which holds the promise of recovery and personal discovery of what makes up a healthy, loving relationship.

Signs of Recovery

In the twelve-step recovery process it is helpful to develop a daily relationship with a higher power (higher-self, better-self, recovery group, spiritual community, higher spirit or God) to assist your efforts to heal from the addiction. We become willing to be vulnerable because the capacity to trust those who are trustworthy is created by our faith in a higher power and meeting trustworthy people. We can surrender, one day at a time, our whole life strategy of, and our obsession with, the pursuit

SLAA Promises

1. We will regain control of our lives.

2. We will begin to feel dignity and respect for ourselves.

3. The loneliness will subside and we will begin to enjoy being alone.

4. We will no longer be plagued by an unceasing sense of longing.

5. In the company of family and friends, we will be with them in body and mind.

6. We will pursue interests and activities that we desire for ourselves.

7. Love will be a committed, thoughtful decision rather than a feeling by which we are overwhelmed.

8. We will love and accept ourselves.

9. We will relate to others from a state of wholeness.

10. We will extend ourselves for the purpose of nurturing our own or another's spiritual growth.

11. We will make peace with our past and make amends to those we have hurt.

12. We will be thankful for what has been given us, what has been taken away, and what has been left behind.

SLAA Online Group of Sex and Love Addicts Anonymous-Readings/ Literature (www.slaaonline.org/readings.html#promises2)

of romantic and sexual intrigue and emotional dependency.

We are restored to sanity, on a daily basis, by participating in this process of recovery. We learn to avoid situations that may put us at risk physically, morally, psychologically, or spiritually. In this process of recovery, it is essential to accept, love, appreciate, and forgive ourselves, take responsibility for our own lives, and take care of our own needs before involving ourselves with others.

In recovery, we become willing to ask for help, allowing ourselves to be vulnerable and learning to trust and accept others as we work through the pain of our low self-esteem and our fears of abandonment and responsibility. We learn to feel comfortable in healthy solitude, and embrace it as a place to get to know and appreciate ourselves. We begin to accept our imperfections and mistakes as part of being human, healing our shame and perfectionism while working on our character defects.

We begin to substitute honesty and authenticity for self-destructive ways of expressing emotions and feelings. We become honest in expressing who we are, our feelings and needs, developing true intimacy in our relationships with ourselves and others.

We learn to value sex as a by-product of sharing, commitment, trust, and cooperation in a partnership.

I don't accept crumbs of love . . .

*I seek a relationship with someone who is affectionate
and loving in a full, healthy way . . .*

*I don't pursue relationship with emotionally
unavailable people . . .*

*I seek a relationship with someone who is emotionally aware,
and expressive of feelings and needs in a respectful way . . .*

The Process

Often in relationships it starts out interesting and then we discover things about each other that are not right. We then become concerned and disappointed. We may go on to end the relationship. Ending a relationship does not have to mean that either person is right or wrong, just different.

Life is like this. We often create possibilities, then reality sets in and efforts fail. That's the way of the world. When we fight this process we get sad. If we accept this process, without negative attachment, we can feel happy again.

BEING	DOING	HAVING
Possibility	Reality	Results
Great ideas	Efforts	What happens
Interesting start up of a relationship	Discovery of differences and disappointments	Ending the relationship
Open	Listening & learning	Transforming our relationship

Our daily state of being is more important then the outcomes. Desired outcomes are elusive and difficult to create.

An Amazing Daily Process

1. I let go, emptying myself, detaching, being a clearing for new possibilities . . .

2. I want, appreciate and love myself . . .

3. I am grateful, thankful, serene, and at peace . . . I keep it simple and clear . . .

4. I am joyful, happy, and optimistic . . . I do what I do in a fun way . . .

5. I am outgoing, loving, compassionate, forgiving, friendly, and kind . . .

6. I am creative and open to new ways, synchronicity, meaningful coincidences, and unforeseen opportunities . . .

7. I am open to synergy, working together, and cooperative action whose outcome is greater than the sum of its parts . . .

8. I share abundance . . .

Couples Work

Much work on couples relationships has been done by researchers, counselors, and workshop leaders, and further information can be discovered at the following sites:

- The Gottman Institute—www.gottman.com/
- The Hendricks Institute—www.therelationshipsolution.com/
- Love Tips—www.marthabeveridge.com

Releasing Regret and Resentment

It is impossible to feel love if you are feeling regretful about your life choices or resentful about people, places, situations, or things. Here is a way to become aware of these emotions and release them. In the first column, fill in the regrets and resentments you have had and still have in your life. In the second column, add the underlying need you relate to that regret or resentment, or the value that you need to uphold to live well with yourself. In the third column, fill in the actions you can take to meet your own needs and live a life you value.

REGRET	NEED YOU HAVE/ VALUE YOU HOLD	ACTION YOU CAN TAKE NOW TO MEET YOUR OWN NEED, LIVE WHAT YOU VALUE

Through Awareness, Acceptance, Appreciation, and Action
you will free yourself from carrying around
the burden of regrets and resentments.

You will be light and free to love . . .

Access the Love within each day . . .

RESENTMENT	NEED YOU HAVE/ VALUE YOU HOLD	ACTION YOU CAN TAKE NOW TO MEET YOUR OWN NEED, LIVE WHAT YOU VALUE

You are being challenged by your partner . . . he or she loses it, expressing stored-up anger and resentment. Instead of becoming angry or defensive as an automatic response, ask yourself, "What need or value is trying to come out, what need or value expression is missing, what action can be taken to help him or her meet that need or live that value?"

Don't hold to anger, hurt, or pain.
They steal your energy and keep you from love.

—LEO BUSCAGLIA

Healing Negative People

Did you ever wonder why good things sometimes happen for bad people and sometimes really good people struggle to find their beloved and create abundance, even though they use affirmations and positive thinking?

I once knew a guy who was extremely negative, yet it seemed like one break after another went his way while I struggled to create what I wanted. He actually took pride in being ornery, negative, cynical, sarcastic, unhappy, and creating animosity. I tried just as hard to be positive as he did to be negative.

What I finally discovered was that a "cycle of nonexpectation" was controlling my beliefs, feelings, and relationships. In the intimate relationship arena, though I really wanted to be with my beloved and create abundance, in my subconscious *I did not really expect it could happen,* because it had not happened in the past. In the same way, I would become convinced that difficult coworkers could never be positive and open to change, because they had refused to be positive in the past.

That was very powerful for me to learn. I also realized that my negative associate was gaining things in his life because he thought he was great and deserved success. But even though he got them, he was always unhappy—because he did not *believe in happiness.* No matter how much he acquired, no matter how many successes he racked up, he would forever remain unhappy with all his accomplishments. *He didn't expect happiness.*

Change Yourself, Not Others

Can anything be done with people who don't value positivity, love, happiness, collaboration? I have found that when I try to change others I get them very annoyed at me. If I try to change them because I think it is "in their best interest," they usually respond with resisting actions and attitudes that essentially say "I am grown up, and I define for myself what is best for me. I don't care what you think. Who are you, to change me?"

I learned that I can not really change others directly. When I make inner changes to myself, however, that forces others to make different choices. So, for example, you can't make your brother-in-law stop smoking, but you can stop pretending that is OK for him to smoke in your home. You might say, "I prefer to not have smoke in my home. I wish people would not smoke for their own benefit, but if they haven't yet stopped smoking, they need to do it outside." This changes the situation. It detaches you from the cat-and-mouse game of "Stop smoking . . ." "No, I don't want to . . ." You can also choose to go deeper and ask yourself: "What is in my own life that I want to give up, but feel addicted to?" It could be a feeling, a thought, a role, a job, a person, a food, TV, the Internet, or some other aspect of your lifestyle. If you look closely you usually will find something you feel you can not live without, something that isn't doing you any good. The other person is mirroring that addicted aspect of yourself back at you, which is why it disturbs you.

People's fears block the natural flow of energy within them. It is like they are in an inner prison of negative thinking. We can only help free the person from their inner tortures by avoiding the inclination to fall back into negativity ourselves. We become clearer each day, one day at a time. We make the most progress when we stop playing "I'm good and you're bad" cat-and-mouse games and clear up our own inner and outer lives.

I have made many changes,
and other people around me have had to change,
but that is very different from me trying to change them.

FRIENDLY LOVE: SWEETNESS AND UNCONDITIONAL LOVE

Unconditional love is simply kindness and friendliness . . .

I have seen that many people keep psychological sweetness from themselves. When they get too close to human sweetness-kindness-warmth, they feel their power to be who they are is threatened, and the emotions of fear and anger come up to create a safe distance again. They may even do something to sabotage their good feelings. They may prefer individualism and solitary rather than team activities. Such people don't do much to create and support teams around them. Companies that have a culture of teams create more collaboration, while companies run by leaders who are not team-oriented do not foster teams in the workplace.

When people start to feel strong feelings of peace, happiness, joy, love, and gratitude, they may not be used to them. They may feel strange and uncomfortable in such a *light and wonderful space,* and they may then do something to get themselves out of that space and back to their comfort zone of turf protection and isolated individualism. They can't imagine how they could remain in charge and get their needs met if they become part of a team, group, or community. It may take them time to get to the point where they can feel comfortable with these wonderful feelings of wellness and well-being.

Each day, through centering and meditation,
you can access the sweetness of the love within . . .
when you feel the love within, you can express
it in acts of kindness, compassion,
and friendliness with others . . .

We all need security, and when we are young we think riches will bring it to us. We may try to marry well, go for the gold, make deals with the devil, and do things in business that are against our own higher values and perhaps unethical. Take care that your own process of creating prosperity and abundance is done in an ethical way.

*I'd rather have roses on my table
than diamonds around my neck.*

—EMMA GOLDMAN

*Too often we underestimate the power
of a touch, a smile, a kind word, a listening ear,
an honest compliment, or the smallest act of caring,
all of which have the potential to turn a life around.*

—LEO BUSCAGLIA

*In conflict,
when you develop the power to be
calm, unconditionally loving and kind,
you demonstrate a concern for
the happiness of the person,
which miraculously melts the conflict.*

Go Beyond Addictions to Love and Power

Habits make or break us. Habits are the patterns of our lives. They add to our wellbeing and prosperity, or they waste our time and squander our resources and potential.

*Bad habits are like a comfortable bed,
easy to get into, but hard to get out of.*

—ANONYMOUS

*Bad habits are like chains that are too light to feel
until they are too heavy to carry.*

—WARREN BUFFETT

Good habits result from resisting temptation.

—ANCIENT PROVERB

A nail is driven out by another nail.
Habit is overcome by habit.
—DESIDERIUS ERASMUS

Habit is either the best of servants
or the worst of masters.
—NATHANIEL EMMONS

Choose the life that is most useful,
and habit will make it the most agreeable.
—FRANCIS BACON

Habit is habit
and not to be flung out of the window by any man,
but coaxed downstairs a step at a time
—MARK TWAIN

A LAST REMINDER ABOUT ANGER, RESENTMENT, AND FORGIVENESS

When you hold resentment toward another,
you are bound to that person or condition
by an emotional link that is stronger than steel.
Forgiveness is the only way to dissolve that link and get free.
—CATHERINE PONDER

When I saw that quote on forgiveness I thought how we need to forgive our former partners, bosses, and coworkers for being the foolish, damaged, obsessed, insensitive people they are.

It will be helpful to detach from their "shenanigans," chaos and drama. A "dry drunk" is someone who learned the pattern of alcoholics from their family. She or he may not be drinking, but is behaving with the same dysfunctional behaviors. We need to avoid similar patterns in our own behavior by being strong enough to not allow our past back into our heads and lives again.

she•nan•i•gan [sh_ nánnig_n] :

1. questionable act: something that is deceitful, underhanded, or otherwise questionable (usually used in the plural);

2. trick or prank: a playful trick, mischievous prank, or other display of high spirits

Unless we forgive the people who hurt us, we carry anger, regrets and resentments that hold us back from experiencing love, light, and full creative expression. We need to forgive, let go, and create the wonderful life we want . . .

We need to do that with all the people in our past and in the present—for example, with the tricksters at work. In Al-Anon, the twelve-step group that helps people deal with the alcoholics in their lives, people are helped to clarify their anger and resentments because the people in our lives who behave in hurtful and ridiculous ways can constantly be upsetting—if we take the bait.

The New Powerful Woman and the Conscious, Loving Man in a Co-Creative, Co-Empowering Relationship

Powerful women need to learn how to relate to powerful, conscious, loving men . . .

Because women were oppressed, and have been fighting for power for so long . . .

when it comes to mating it is hard for them to share, love, and co-create with a man in a compassionate, gentle, co-empowering way.

—SANDY HINDEN

	I'M NOT OK— NEGATIVE VIEW OF SELF	I'M OK— POSITIVE VIEW OF SELF
	Uncertain relationship	Positive, secure relationship
	Childhood abandonment	Healing and skills* work done by both partners
	Adult love seeker	The presence of the Beloved
You're OK Positive View of Partner	**I'm not OK, you're OK:** Negative self-image and positive image of your partner—THAWING-WARMING	**I'm OK, you're OK:** Positive self-image and image of your partner—WARM & LOVING
	You feel DEPENDENT and appear to be needy and clingy.	You are INTERDEPENDENT and feel secure and safe, alone or with your partner. Being with your partner soothes you. You feel like you are in a safe harbor and emotionally recharge each other.
	When you are separated from your partner you may feel upset and anxious. You are not confident about your partner's love for you and may keep seeking it.	You are autonomous and confident when you go out on your own. You are confident your partner will be there appreciatively upon your return.
	Fearful and avoidant	Avoidant relationship
	Childhood abuse and abandonment	Childhood abuse
You're Not OK Negative View of Partner	Absence of appreciation, warmth and love	Adult love avoider
	I'm not OK, you're not OK: Negative image of yourself and others—COLD	**I'm OK, you're not OK:** Positive self-image and negative image of your partner—COOL
	You are COUNTER-DEPENDENT, untrusting of yourself and many others. Though you want to be close, you run away when warmth is offered.	You feel INDEPENDENT, and don't share your feelings of sadness, fear, or anger. To deal with your hurt, you may distance yourself, appear preoccupied, and focus on work.

* Three Emotional Love Skills
1. Learn to take care of your feelings and needs.
2. Learn to appreciate yourself and your partner.
3. Learn to communicate and listen to feelings and needs nonjudgmentally.

CHAPTER 3

Physical Love

Physical love takes place through the senses of sound, sight, smell, taste, and touch.

We are stimulated and enjoy what we are experiencing. Physically we can enjoy sex, food, sports, and our surroundings in our home, community, nature, travel, and viewing the cosmos.

Physical enjoyment takes time. To enjoy requires you to be present and savor the experience.

The way to enjoyment is in letting go of time and becoming one with the experience. These pleasures can excite us and refresh us. The key to healthy living is doing them in the right proportion to everything else that you need to do in life.

Unhealthy addictive pleasures become attractive to us when we are not fulfilling our basic need for healthy love, touch, warmth and sexual expression.

So many of us do not have our basic need for healthy love, touch, warmth, and sexual expression met with a loving partner. In their absence, feelings of loneliness, boredom, or insecurity can result in addictive behavior. We need to learn to provide healthy love, touch, warmth, and sexual expression for ourselves. We need to take the time to be loving, gentle, and sweet with ourselves. This is so foreign to us in our society, which urges us to race around and promotes being unconscious, denying our feelings, and being out of touch with ourselves. It is important to identify our own feelings; to step back each day and ask ourselves:

- Did I lose something today?
- Do I feel abandoned in anyway? By whom?
- Do I feel disappointed?
- Do I feel rejected?
- Do I feel manipulated, subjugated, dominated?
- Do I feel fear?
- Do I feel disregarded, ignored, neglected, or diminished?
- Do I feel numb?
- Do I feel hungry?
- Do I feel angry or resentful?
- Do I feel lonely?
- Do I feel tired?
- Do I feel sad?
- Do I feel confused?
- Do I feel stuck?

If you recognize any of the above feelings in yourself, you need to be careful that you do not succumb to addictive, unhealthy pleasures to avoid the pain these feeling can create. The addiction can be to food, shopping, gambling, sex, porn, drugs, smoking, or even exercise.

We need to find healthy ways
to meet our need to get to positive inner feelings of
peace, serenity, warmth, love, joy, and happiness each day.

HEALING FROM SEX ADDICTION TO REAL LOVE

Porn Nation is a book written by Michael Leahy, a man who spent over twenty-five years as a recreational user and big fan of pornography before he discovered what experts call the "crack cocaine of sexual addiction:" Internet porn. Leahy states that pornography is a $100 billion a year industry worldwide, more than all the professional sports combined, yet open discussion of pornography and sex addiction is still taboo. Easily accessible through the Internet, its anonymity brings the average teen 14,000 sexual images and messages annually.

All of the following statistics are taken from the Family Safe Media website: www.familysafemedia.com/pornography_statistics. html.

Who uses pornography?

- 42.7% of Internet users view pornography
- Worldwide visitors to pornographic websites: 72 million

Children

- The average age of first Internet exposure to pornography: eleven years old (www.internet-filter-review. toptenreviews.com).

- Nine out of ten children aged between the ages of eight and sixeen have viewed pornography on the Internet, in most cases unintentionally (London School of Economics, January 2002).

Men

- Over 70 percent of men between eighteen and thirty-four visited a porn site in a typical month. (ComScore, 2004)

- A 1996 Promise Keepers survey at one of their stadium events revealed that over 50 percent of the men in attendance were involved with pornography within one week of attending the event.

Women

- 28 percent of those admitting to sexual addiction are women (www.internet-filter-review.toptenreviews.com).

- 34 percent of female readers of *Today's Christian Woman's* online newsletter admitted to intentionally accessing Internet porn in a recent poll, and one out of every six women, including Christians, struggles with an addiction to pornography (*Today's Christian Woman,* Fall 2003)

- Women struggling with pornography addiction: 17 percent (www.internet-filter-review.toptenreviews.com).

- One in three visitors to adult websites are women (www.internet -filter-review. toptenreviews.com)

Clergy

- 33 percent of clergy admitted to having visited a sexually explicit website. Of those who had visited a porn site, 53 percent had visited such sites "a few times" in the past year, and 18 percent visit sexually explicit sites between a couple of times a month and more than once a week. (*Christianity Today* survey, 2000)

Revenue

- The total pornography industry revenue for 2006: $13.3 billion in the United States; $97 billion worldwide (www.internet -filter-review.toptenreviews.com).

Consequences

- 47 percent of families said pornography is a problem in their home (Focus on the Family poll, October 1, 2003, www.focus onthefamily.com)

- At a 2003 meeting of the American Academy of Matrimonial

Lawyers, two-thirds of the 350 divorce lawyers who attended said the Internet played a significant role in divorces in the past year, with excessive interest in online porn contributing to more than half such cases. Pornography had an almost non-existent role in divorce just seven or eight years ago. (www. divorcewizards.com)

Sex is such a powerful dimension of human existence. The Internet is a powerful, affordable, easily accessible global tool. Put the power of instant availability of Internet access together with something as deep and profound as human sexuality, and you have a toxic combination.

Michael Leahy is the founder of Bravehearts LLC, an organization dedicated to helping people lead healthy sexual lives. He knows there can be bigger consequences to porn addiction than spending time and money. He founded the organization after his life had been negatively affected by his addiction to pornography when his addiction to porn led him to have an affair that caused a divorce from his wife of fifteen years, "My fantasy life sort of grew legs. . . ."

Leahy tells audiences that pornography is based in falsehood—an illusion, not a reality. Sex can be an extremely powerful component of a healthy relationship, but pornography alters that by causing people to view individuals as body parts, not people. A calm dialogue about pornography is needed because there is a cultural taboo about openly discussing it. People need to be educated about porn before they saturate themselves in it and become addicted to it.

He offers a sex survey at www.mysexsurvey.com to see if you are addicted to pornography.

Pornography addiction may make people feel shameful about themselves until they develop a callousness about it and tell themselves it is OK to be a "recreational user." Like being a "recreational user" of drugs and gambling, they see nothing wrong with it. They may not be aware, or deny, that it has any personal, family, or social side effects—such as addiction, family divorce, or porno industry-related AIDS.

Like many compulsive behaviors, porn addiction is usually a secret addiction. Even respectable members of the community may have their time, productivity, and self-esteem squandered by hours viewing porn.

What Human Need Does Porn Fill?

Most people need to feel the sexual release, peace, love, respect, joy, bliss, and ecstasy that orgasm can bring. Sex is very powerful. It temporarily suspends your thinking, which is a miracle in and of itself. When you experience orgasm you don't think for a few seconds, and all the cares, troubles, and catastrophes of the world disappear from the inner voice and screen of the mind. So, it is no wonder that people keep seeking sexual and pornographic pleasure. They enjoy ecstasy for a few moments. So, in the absence of a healthy, loving sexual relationship, porn substitutes as a way to gain access to pure pleasure, and an escape from painful realities of daily losses, abandonment, disappointment, rejections, hunger, anger, loneliness, and even tiredness.

Uncomfortable communication: Pornography can also take place in relationships, when a partner is uncomfortable communicating what he or she wants sexually and substitutes the pornographic representation of it for the real thing because they cannot bring themselves to ask for it.

Fear of deeper intimacy: A partner may fear what would happen if they did ask for what they wanted sexually and actually got it. They would be uncomfortable with the new level of intimacy in the new sexual activities.

Masking another thought: Obsessively and compulsively using porn by surfing from one porn site to the next for hours on end can be a way to mask another issue that is disturbing to think about. The pornography provides an escape from the painful thought or realization, i.e., feelings of loss, rejection, conflict, worry.

Numbing the pain of daily life: In the absence of real passion and intimacy, feelings of loneliness, boredom, or insecurity can all result in porn addiction. Pornography provides easy access to pain relief and high-energy excitement, numbing daily pains. It can be used to escape reality but in the long run, like any addiction, it worsens the reality you are trying to escape by causing secondary problems, i.e., in relationships or job performance.

Returning to a safe, comfortable, familiar place: If you used pornography as child or young teenager you may have become used to being in the "porn zone," where you felt the excitement of using porn, then had an orgasm, and then felt guilt or shame afterwards. Your emotional barometer became set to this excitement-orgasm-guilt-shame emotional trio. Using porn today can take you back to that original emotional state you may find familiar. If you are uncomfortable feeling too much joy, love, and warmth you may use porn to bring yourself down to a state of shame and guilt again. This has been called "repression of the sublime."

Secondary Problems Created by Porn Addiction

Addiction availability: Pornography is easily available and is a powerful self-medication that enables us to relieve pain with pleasure. We may find that we return to it year after year. Pornography is always available in your private places. You can go for days, weeks, or months without using porn and then you may find yourself back into it again. You may trick yourself into believing that you are not really hooked and addicted. You think you will just view it for a few minutes, just today. Wham, you become entranced again. You find you are back in the grip of this self-sabotaging cycle. Life ceaselessly creates daily joy, suffering, and pain. We all need to learn how to practice detaching from suffering and pain and heal ourselves in a healthy way, each day and each night.

Work, home, and community trouble: People can get in trouble with pornography at work, in their intimate relationships, or in the community. At work, if they are lucky, their employer may just give them a warning when they are caught using porn. They may then try to stop, but because they are addicted, they start again and get caught again. They may then get fired or be told to go for counseling. In the family, pornography can become a serious problem when the addiction comes to light. When the partner finds out, he or she may give an ultimatum to the other partner or silently feel abandoned and withdraw love from the relationship. In the community, it can ruin your reputation if you are a leader of a business or a civic or religious organization.

Numbing and jading effect: Pornography addiction may keep you from appreciating the subtleties of life and from communicating in a friendly way with men, women, children, and the elderly. It can lower your enthusiasm and joy for life.

Wasting time, energy, money, and potential: Pornography addiction has a hypnotic effect and can grab and then lock your attention. It can lead you to waste hours on the Internet when you could be spending the time productively with family, friends, or community members; at work, developing new ideas, businesses, books, and products; exercising, walking in nature, and enjoying hobbies.

Each day we experience daily joy, suffering, and pain. From hour to hour we can practice detaching from suffering and pain and heal ourselves in a healthy way, avoiding any addiction, including pornography, as a substitute for the pleasure of real love.
Through daily prayer and meditation, talking to friends about our feelings and needs, and learning to take good care of our feelings and needs each day and night we can experience being whole, powerful, loving, and creative. Through self-love, love for others, and love for the world, nature, the cosmos, and the creation-creator, we can become whole and healed in our consciousness and heart. Instead of passively watching a glowing screen of images for hours and hours again this evening, participate in something that will utilize your physical abilities, warm your heart, or challenge your mind . . . go for a walk or a bike ride, play a game of simple sports like tossing a ball, read a good book, magazine, or newspaper instead. Better yet, be active with a friend, family member, or community organization.

PEACEFUL PASSION WITHOUT PERFORMANCE ANXIETY

Sex can be anxiety provoking if it triggers performance anxiety. Peaceful passion is a process of using love and touch without being concerned about having to experience orgasm. The partners recognize each other's value and simply enjoy genital closeness without pressure to perform. By gently caressing, with no goal other than to be warm with each other, the pressure is off. What may start out as softness may become stronger, but that is not the goal. Gently caressing each other's genitals and genital to genital togetherness is soothing and loving, reassuring that you are truly loved. Gently touching, kissing, and holding is very pleasant and comforting as the two of you create a world of love for each other to enjoy.

> The message we give our bodies—
> one of irritation or acceptance—
> is the message to which our bodies will answer.
>
> —DEB SHAPIRO, *YOUR BODY SPEAKS YOUR MIND*

It is important to overcome emotional and physical numbness, distancing, disconnection, and isolation that may have replaced warmth and love.

You and your partner can return to a sense of sexual innocence and establish and respect healthy boundaries in yourself and each other. From a secure experience of boundaries you can experience and manage feelings of vulnerability while staying open to pleasure and the sweetness of love.

This can be done thorough inner appreciation and communication and by reclaiming your natural sexual innocence, joy, and the comfortable bliss of gentle caress.

Peaceful passion is the gateway to viewing your partner as your beloved.

See more at www.intimacy.retreats.com.

GARDENING, COOKING, HOME DESIGN, COMMUNITY BEAUTIFICATION, EARTH REPAIR

> I sing the body electric.
>
> —WALT WHITMAN

How we work at anything determines how we feel each day.

• Are we stressed, and do we strain all the time?

- Are we intense and super busy, too busy to smell the roses or the coffee?

- Are we too busy to become involved in something new that would be very beneficial for us or others?

Many of life's joys can be experienced in hobbies such as gardening, cooking, home design, community beautification, earth repair projects, and sports.

Our appreciation for them opens our heart further. So many people are hurt, isolated, and lonely. By becoming involved in gardening, cooking, home design, community beautification, earth repair projects, and sports they can feel good about them themselves and share their love for the projects and activities with others. Others will come to appreciate their expertise and enjoy the fruits of the labors. Love will grow within and between people.

Appreciation Opens the Heart

- Be careful not to become obsessive about any activity . . .

- Keep it in balance with the rest of your life responsibilities . . .

- True love grows with ease and joy . . . .

- Love is not overattachment and addiction . . .

- Love nourishes happiness . . .

- Gently and easily enjoy more of what you do each day . . .

- Talk to neighbors, colleagues, or friends . . .

- Go for a walk . . .

- Appreciate your surroundings, and if they need it, see how you might improve them . . .

- Be grateful for what you have and for the opportunity to contribute to making a difference around you . . .

Our hearts are the emotional centers of our bodies,
and they put out frequencies that are ten times
the power of the frequencies of our brains . . .
When we are happy, we vibrate at a higher frequency
than when we are angry or sad . . .
Experiencing physical, emotional, and mental stillness
harmonizes the vibrational output of the body,
heart, and mind and we become stronger.

—JOHN ROBSON (WWW.HIGHERAWARENESS.COM)

Practicing the art of self-appreciation, self-love, and self-sweetness each day is the path to well-being. Only by taking the time to quiet our self each day to access our inner pain can we heal our pain with self-love and self-sweetness.

It is a paradox.

Only by accessing
our inner pain to
***recognize** it,*
***process** it*
and
***detach** from it*
each day
can we
heal it
and access
***inner pleasures** of*
serenity,
love,
sweetness,
gratitude,
*and **happiness**.*

*It is the act of forgiveness that opens up the only possible
way to think creatively about the future at all.*

—FATHER DESMOND WILSON

Holding on to old regrets, angers, and resentments keeps our creative energy trapped, stifled, and stuck. Each day we can experience dreams and endless possibilities. We are only limited by a lack of belief and hope, in others and ourselves, and by our doubt, fear, guilt, shame, regrets, and resentments. Each day we can begin again on a clean page in our book of life. We can find new freedom by practicing the art of forgiveness. Each day, we can forgive ourselves and others, past and present. This way we enter the day free from the past. Almost nothing can really hurt us in the present when we have the key of daily forgiveness. Nothing a friend, boss, or enemy says is worth the emotional price of ongoing resentment. When people create chaos, drama, and hurtful comments, we can choose to not bite the bait, not react defensively, not to get drawn into the animosity, and not automatically fight back. We can give ourselves a gift of freedom by remaining calm, centered, aware, compassionate, and forgiving, and focus on solutions, possibilities, and what we want to create. It is our choice—regrets, anger, and resentment, or freedom and power to create possibilities. We can forgive everyone and anything, past and present, that distracts us from our creative power.

Growing Love around the Planet . . .
One Garden at a Time

One of the best ways to feel physical love for life is to grow a garden. Adults and children can find inner peace, love for nature, and understanding of how earth, nutrients, air, sun, and water—how needs, seeds, weeds, and deeds—interact to create a bounty.

In the 1980s, I started a program called Universal Children's Gardens. It is now being re-launched worldwide as Children's Mother Earth Gardens.

You can learn more about Children's Mother Earth Gardens at www.worldcmeg.org.

Children's Mother Earth Gardens

Mission

❀ To grow peace, friendship and compassion between local and global children of the world

❀ To foster the growth of food, flowers, trees & love for nature

❀ To protect the earth, trees, air & waters of the world

❀ To enjoy the garden, each other & celebrate life

My garden is my
most beautiful masterpiece.

—CLAUDE MONET

Kind hearts are the garden,
Kind thoughts are the roots,
Kind words are the flowers,
Kind deeds are the fruits,
Take care of your garden
And keep out the weeds,
Fill it with sunshine
Kind words and kind deeds.

—HENRY WADSWORTH LONGFELLOW

The Eastern tradition of aesthetics and ethics
places nature and its environment at the
same level the Western counterparts do for their
religious/spiritual and historical scenes.

To the Chinese or the Japanese artist,
the placement of a rock in a garden or in
a painting touches upon the divine.

—MANKH (WALTER E. HARRIS, III)
HAIKU TEACHER, POET, AND ESSAYIST

Adult gardeners can explore more love for nature through Gardens for Humanity at www.gardensforhumanity.org.

Physical love can be expressed through the joy of gardening with family, friends, and neighbors in a garden on a farm for inner city children to visit, in community gardens in urban neighborhoods, in backyard gardens in the suburbs, in a school garden, in a religious education program garden, or in an apartment near a window. Wherever you grow your garden, let it be a magical expression of your love for yourself, others, and the whole world. The healing magic will be felt within your heart and show up as a twinkle in your eyes.

We are stardust,
Billion year old carbon,
We are golden,
And we've got to get ourselves
back to the garden.

—JONI MITCHELL, "WOODSTOCK"

We must cultivate our garden.

—VOLTAIRE, *CANDIDE* (1759)

To know of someone
here and there whom we accord with,
who is living on with us, even in silence—
this makes our earthly ball a peopled garden.

—JOHANN WOLFGANG VON GOETHE

Our garden ... is my world.
Mine, the hills, the seas.
Mine is the whole world!
To chase! To skip!
To roam! To loll!
To soar like a dove!
To dance! To love

—NINA GLEKIVA, A RUSSIAN CHILD AGE 6, 1999

CHAPTER 4

Family Love

. . . escape from my own ego-based desires, selfish inclinations, and the 'me first' mentality that ultimately cause pain in my life. In their place, I gain life's true and lasting gifts—family, friendship, and fulfillment.

—Yehuda Berg

A FAMILY OF LOVE

Love . . . children . . . family love . . . parents' love for children and each other . . . communication . . . shared values, interests, goals, and dreams . . . communication . . . sharing . . . caring . . . struggling . . . deeper conversation . . . humor . . . more love . . . laughing . . . crying . . . dying . . . grieving . . . appreciating . . . hoping . . . praying . . . deeper loving . . . returning to love . . .

LOVE'S PROMISE VS. LOVE'S BROKEN DREAMS

Why does one out of every two of us end up in divorce? We may find ourselves in second and third marriages, some of which also end in divorce. And many of those who stay in marriages are often unhappy, or addicted to porn, or having affairs, or just suffering in quiet desperation, eating, drinking, shopping, or gambling themselves into excitement or oblivion. What is really going on here? What is wrong with this picture of love and family? After the train wreck of our deepest relationships, we may ask: "Where did it all go wrong?"

Trying to understand it all, I pieced the following together from many sources.

CAUSES OF UNHAPPY MARRIAGE AND DIVORCE	CAUSES OF HEALTHY AND HAPPY MARRIAGE
PERSONALITY TRAITS	
Controlling	Collaboration Skills
Inflexible	Flexible and able to change
Irrational	Rational and reasonable
Harsh	Compassionate
Lack of communication	Communication skills
Inability to manage or resolve conflict	Conflict resolution skills
Self-centered, arrogant	Mutual appreciation and respect
Inconsistency	Consistency
Lack of integrity, doesn't do what is said	Integrity, does what is said
Sarcasm and cynicism	Healthy sense of humor
Belittling each other dreams	Sharing and working on dreams
VALUES AND EXPECTATIONS	
Differing over	**Resolving conflict through**
Household tasks	Communicating feelings and needs and making clear requests. See Nonviolent (compassionate) communication (www.cnvc.org).
Having or rearing children	
Sticking to traditional roles	
Allowing room for personal growth	Coordinating different dreams and goals.
Culture and lifestyle	
Religious beliefs	
Sexuality	
Interference from parents or in-laws	
Personal and career goals	

RESULTS	
Selfish fighting	Giving, sharing, generosity
Lack of commitment to the marriage	Commitment to the partner and the marriage
Intellectual incompatibility	Having meaningful conversations
Alcohol addiction, substance abuse, or other addictive behavior	Healthy habits
Infidelity, Dishonesty	Integrity
Abandonment	Intimacy (into–me–you–see)
Physical Abuse	Compassion
Sexual Abuse	Tenderness
Emotional Abuse	Sweetness
Personality differences or "irreconcilable differences"	Appreciating each other's differences
Inability to deal with each other's petty idiosyncrasies	Getting feedback
Lack of maturity	Willingness to change and improve
Criminal behavior and incarceration for crime	Willingness to learn healthy ways to live
Financial problems	Talking openly about money and willingness to work together to create abundance
Falling out of love	Making time to be loving and romantic
Mental instability or mental illness	Willingness to seek help to change and grow

How Did So Many of Us Go Into Marriage So Unprepared?

Communications: Imagine that you get a job in a nuclear reactor and no one trains you what to do or say day to day, or in an emergency? Even healthy people can become volatile in close quarters, and no one trained you how to be a mediator, or a negotiator, or how to fight fairly when things get tough. Marriages can turn nuclear within a few years of the gala wedding and luxury honeymoon on the tropical island. Marriage without skills? Yikes!

Raising the Young: Imagine that you are a school teacher working with little kids and you have to teach and guide them how to behave appropriately and creatively. And imagine that you never went to school to learn how to teach. You are pretty young, without a lot of life experience, and all of a sudden you find yourself in front of children pretending to be a teacher. You would probably be a pretty crummy teacher, given the challenge of a complicated society and what children have to master to be a success in this life. Parenting without preparation? Yikes—Part II!

Dream Catching: Finally, the vast majority of people can't manipulate the capitalist or communist system, they can't control group dynamics in the workplace, and they can't control other people's addictions, procrastination or out-of-control behavior. They are not trained to be a shaman, a psychic mind reader, a healer, or a dream catcher. Yet every person has a dream, and head-on dream collisions occur in family settings every day. Surrounded by cultural and economic forces that can be out of control themselves, we are not trained to be able to manifest our individual and shared dreams under one roof. No one trained us to be intrapsychic healers or interpersonal and community shaman. Yet our dreams want to be realized in the difficult world we all find ourselves. Our dreams, the inner core of our existence, can be laughed at in the workplace, but when they are laughed at and stomped on by our so-called loved ones, that is too much to take. Destroying each other's dreams? Yikes—Part III!

So we are just not prepared to communicate, raise the young, or catch our dreams and manifest them as couples. Marital bliss dissipates. We are not trained to deal with what happens when problems arise. The skills are just not there for us unless we embark on an amazing journey of skills training for multidimensional family life in a modern world.

Love is perfect kindness.

—JOSEPH CAMPBELL

LOVE FOR THE CHILDREN IN OUR FAMILIES AND THE WORLD

Family life! The United Nations is child's play compared to the tugs and splits and need to understand and forgive in any family.

—MAY SARTON

When you are faced with a child, a love partner, or elder parent who is having a temper tantrum seek to discover what he or she needs. Be deeply yielding and receptive. Instead of giving into your own frustration and anger, stop being rigid and deeply understand. *Relax, yield, listen, and understand.* People often are frustrated but don't articulate what they feel or need. Don't slip into being angry; it will only create distance and make it impossible for the suffering person to open up to you. Achieve deeper receptivity through conscious relaxation, patience, endurance, and steadfastness. The way to make our children, our partners, and our parents patient and loving is to be that way ourselves.

LIFESTYLE AND CHARACTER TRAITS

I have observed that there seems to be seven economic situations in life. Each has its own set of experiences and needs. Each has its pitfalls, trials, and tribulations. Each affects our children.

1. **Poverty:** Survival

2. **Lower Income:** Time constraints, conflict, complaining

3. **Lower-Middle Income:** Time constraints, conflict, complaining

4. **Middle Income:** Time constraints, inauthenticity, cynicism

5. **Upper-Middle Income:** Time constraints, disconnect from the general public to distinguish oneself

6. **Upper Income:** Freedom to disconnect from general society

7. **Great Wealth:** Others raise our children, can become selfish and greedy

Each of us develops a lifestyle and various character traits we are aware of and not aware of. We each have some blind spots that we don't see or are in denial about. The fastest way to creating a better life is to:

1. See what we are doing wrong, through:
   - self-reflection
   - casually listening to what others say about us in humor or remarks
   - asking people for their direct feedback about how they see us

2. Get to know ourselves better

3. Letting go of our old patterns of thinking, feelings, words, and behaviors-actions, and creating new patterns

4. Growing stronger each day

There seem to be two mindsets that lead to the way we feel and treat our children and other's children. Where are you? Take the *Family Attitudes Inventory* below. Check off where you are on the continuum for each quality-character trait.

FAMILY ATTITUDES INVENTORY											
	1	2	3	4	5	6	7	8	9	10	
Hateful											Loving
Harsh											Nurturing
Judgmental											Accepting
Cold, unfriendly											Warm, friendly
Uncaring											Caring
Inconsiderate											Considerate
Foolish											Wise
Inconsistent											Consistent
Neglectful											Supportive
Vengeful											Forgiving
Hurtful											Compassionate

The clearer people think, the better they feel, the kinder the words they say and the more constructive the actions they take. The better they think, feel, communicate, and behave, the more they create harmony with their children, partners, neighbors, and coworkers. The more harmony they create in the world. Thus, we can change the world by helping people change their thinking.

I have seen families who were very successful financially hurt each other greatly. They probably had unresolved issues, incomplete closures, and unexpressed pain and grief, and became untrusting and unloving with each other. They hurt each other back and forth. They were each trying to succeed yet had a hard time collaborating as a family. Each had been hurt by the others, so the hurt got passed round and round. They were all highly educated but were unable to be loving and kind with each other.

There seemed to be a basic process operating in relationships. If you were hurt badly as a child, your original unhealed hurt would lead to unhappiness and acting in hurtful ways. On the other hand, if you were loved as a child then your inner core would be loving. You were more likely to be peaceful with people, happier within and with others, and to act with kindness to yourself and those around you.

Inner hurt core	$\longrightarrow$	Inner loving core
Animosity, hating and agitation	$\longrightarrow$	Peace and serenity
Unhappiness	$\longrightarrow$	Happiness and joy
Hurtfulness to others	$\longrightarrow$	Kindness to others

I was very pained by the people in these unhappy families. I wanted to help them and suggested they meet with each other to create a better communication process. I suggested they could resolve their disputes and disagreements respectfully and recommended mediation/facilitation to:

- reduce obstacles to communication
- "hear each other out"
- define and clarify issues
- explore possible solutions
- reach a mutually satisfactory agreement

I encouraged them to be on the same team and praised them for their good work. I offered my assistance to all of them in a genuine sense of cooperation. The process is underway. They needed to create a completely new "win-win" communication process of being respectful, friendly, encouraging, praising, cooperative, and trusting, providing open information flow, authenticity, integrity, responsiveness, and vital support. They needed to learn to create and respect each other's boundaries and that it is not OK to be disrespectful to each other every time they disagreed, and it is OK to disagree with each other in a respectful way—agreeing to disagree. Respectful disagreement is a key.

I have seen that healthy disagreement actually leads to "additive solutions" that can be better than when everyone agrees out of fear of disagreement. Healthy disagreement can reveal weakness in a plan and can lead to accommodating each other's feelings and needs.

NO BOUNDARIES	HEALTHY BOUNDARIES
Disrespectful	Respectful
Unfriendly	Friendly
Belittling, discouraging	Encouraging
Ridicule, put-downs	Praising
Win-lose	Win-win
Competition	Cooperation
Untrusting	Trusting
Closed, concealed	Open information flow
Disingenuous	Authenticity, integrity
Rejecting, unresponsiveness	Responsiveness
Nonsupportive	Providing vital support
Controlling	Collaborating
Denying each other's feelings and needs	Accommodating each other's feeling and needs

DYSFUNCTIONAL AND FANTASTIC FAMILIES

The counselor John Bradshaw estimated that 95 percent of us grew up in dysfunctional environments. He presents that children are curious and are natural risk takers. They have lots of courage and venture out into a world that is immense and dangerous. The child initially trusts life and the processes of life. They can be like natural Zen masters; their world is brand new in each and every moment. But, then something happens that convinces children they are not artists, adventurers, and lovers of life. He reminds us that the more we know about how we lost our spontaneous wonder and creativity, the more we can find ways to get them back. Recovery begins with embracing our pain and taking the risk to share it with others. We can do this by joining a group and talking about our pain. He also reminds us that it is OK to make mistakes. Mistakes are our teachers—they help us to learn.

> *Your journey has molded you for your greater good,*
> *and it was exactly what it needed to be.*
> *Don't think that you've lost time.*
> *There is no short-cutting to life. It took each*
> *and every situation you have encountered*
> *to bring you to the now. And now is right on time.*
>
> —ASHA TYSON

Often, people hold on to a story about dysfunctional parents or siblings who abused, neglected, or abandoned them. We need to do the work to get over it. If we were in a family where we were abused, neglected, or abandoned, and we carry around painful baggage about our hurtful parents, we need to heal and let go. Carrying around all that baggage won't allow us to go very far or enjoy life very much, no matter how many achievements and possession we attain.

We need to have no regrets. Through increasing awareness we realize we can learn from all past experiences. This letting go of the past and realization that we can learn from every life situation allows us to rebuild our trust and supports our being more open and once again daring to experience life as it unfolds. We then have the power to co-create our life experience each day by being proactive and creating win-win situations all around us.

Master the art of paying attention to what is happening right now and in each moment and you will discover that life continually brings opportunities to heal your original, past wounds.

The next message you need is right where you are.
—RAM DASS

If a painful memory comes to your awareness, take time to feel it fully. Have empathy, compassion, and forgiveness for yourself and any one else involved. Allow the feelings to transform and the energy to release. By practicing daily this way, we heal the past in the present and become free to connect fully with people and life all around us. Your awareness is the magical key that will open the door to all change; you then can go into a quiet, reflective inner space to discover who you really are and develop the self-trust, self-compassion, and self-forgiveness that will heal you. You will then be open to discovering your power to co-create win-win situations in the present moment.

Family situations are like the weather—
sometime calm, sometime rocky/stormy.
Without the rocky/stormy truths for transformation
and clarity would sink to the murky bottom—
so it's all good no matter what it looks like.
In time—forgiveness blossoms.
—PAULA TEPEDINO

YOUR OLD UNFULFILLING LIFE	YOUR NEW LIFE OF AMAZING POSSIBILITIES
Original hurts Denial Attachment to the past and your interpretation of what happened Negative perceptions	Healing through self empathy, compassion, and forgiveness of yourself and others Letting go of the past Mindful awareness in the present Creating new possibilities every day

Ongoing feelings of:
  Fear
  Guilt
  Shame
  Doubt
	Creating feelings of being:
	  Empowered
	  Friendly, loving and kind
	  Joyful

Negative, undermining Destructive win-lose games	Positive, creative Co-creating win-win situations and synergies
Resistance to change Resistance to positivity Resistance to love Resistance to connection and relationship Resistance to authenticity Resistance to happiness, joy, peace, serenity, and creativity Resistance to the sublime and ecstatic Suppression of the sublime-divine	Building trust Exploring positive feelings and thoughts
Being icy Executive "ice cubes" Craving power and control Being Isolated Hoarding	Creating community through warm, open relationships and authentic communication Agreeing to disagree respectfully and creating bigger, additive solutions that include each other's needs

YOUR OLD UNFULFILLING LIFE	YOUR NEW LIFE OF AMAZING POSSIBILITIES
Cold	Building a culture of teams
Disconnected, dissociated	Open, flowing, authentic, respectful communication
Arrogant and self-satisfied	
Competitive	
Hurt and hurtful	
Using little energy and staying in the safety zone	Using energy and enthusiasm to cross the line into new dimensions and ways of being, doing, and transformation
Hiding and pretending	Clarifying emerging directions, life signs, writing on the wall
Creating a facade that all is okay	Being authentic and in integrity
Bitterness	Sweetness, joy
Squashing the creative spirit in yourself and others	The lifting and elevation of spirit—yours and others
Not listening for others feelings and needs	Listening for others feelings and needs
Not honoring others feelings and needs	Honoring others feelings and needs
Isolated or repetitively hanging out with old cronies with the inability to make new friends and deepen relationships	Integrity and the openness to build new relationships and friendships, and to deepen old friendships

The three most powerful words: I love you.
the four most powerful words: I'm proud of you.

TONY PRICE, AUTHOR

The love, comfort, care, and guidance we habitually provide for our children will come back to create the world we live in. The children are the world of the future.

Our love will be carried into the future through the children. Be the love you want to see in the world. Be kind and thoughtful in your words.

Your words can be destructive poison, healing medicine, or creative potions. Words can be weapons or wisdom. You can become a Master of Animosity or a Healer for Love.

You have the power to create a loving, empowering context for your life each morning and each evening in your meditation and prayer. By setting your context for living to be loving and empowering you will create the best possible life you can.

You will be nurturing to the children and for changing your part of the world, in yourself, the home, the workplace, and the community.

In conflict with family members, when we develop the power to be calm, unconditionally loving, and kind, we demonstrate a concern for the happiness of our partner, parent, or child that miraculously melts the conflict and allows the person to feel safe.

Ultimately, when more and more of us become aware of this *power to be unconditionally loving in conflict* we can transform the world . . . humanity will create *One Love, One Family, One World.*

FILIAL LOVE—LOVE FOR PARENTS AND CARE FOR ELDERS IN OUR SOCIETY

How do we think about our elders?
Old, cranky, not up to date, outmoded,
or do we see them as wise, loving, and worthy of respect . . .

In some cultures around the world care giving to elders is a part of life. "Filial piety," is the value of respect for our family, especially our elders. This comes from the remembrance that without our elders, we would not be here. We owe them our lives and are grateful for their gifting us with life.

Caregiving Cultures

Around the world, caregiving can be a natural occurrence in some cultures where it is possible for families to stay together. Parents may move in with their children and help raise their childrens' children. When the parents themselves need care, their children are prepared to care for them until the end of their life.

Caregiving is these multigenerational families is not seen as a chore or a new role but rather another step in the continuous life of a family. The process reoccurs every generation as parents become grandparents and their children become parents. There is an appreciation of every child and each graduation in the cycle. Family members maintain physically close ties with their parents and grandparents. Seniors are respected and honored.

In some families, as a family grows too big for the house, the sons and daughters move next door, staying as close as they can to their original family. Grandfathers and grandmothers are important to children; they teach them all the lessons and rules for life and great love can pass between grandchildren and grandparents. When the grandparents help the grandchildren, the grandchildren want to help them also.

Historically, in some places in the world, families stayed together no matter how big they grew. When there were larger families, they started their own villages, with the eldest grandfather and grandmother leading the rest. In contemporary societies, we can no longer do that, but we can keep the love and respect alive in other ways. We need to take care of each other when it is needed: children take care of their aging parents and grandparents can help take care of grandchildren.

Close Families, Distant Families

In traditional households, moving far away from family may not be the norm. In the past, in close families, you were not expected to separate from your parents, and care giving is a normal process in the grand scheme of life. Children born into these cultures expect to do as their parents did, and as their parents' parents did before them.

The parents remember that without their parents they would not be here, and without them being here, their children would not be alive. When life is looked at that way, we all owe the world to the elders and family is the most important thing people can have. Ideally grandparents, parents, and grandchildren can trust, love, and depend on each other. The family, and each family member, is seen as sacred.

Many of us no longer have the capability to be close to our parents, yet honoring these traditions can be the foundation of a strong family even if we are apart. We can honor and value our elders whether or not we become caregivers to our parents. If we do bring our aging parents into our homes, we can show our children the value of respecting those that gave us life, and learn the wisdom of our elders together, as a family, growing stronger.

The two most magical
words in the world—
respect and love.

A GLOBAL FAMILY OF FRIENDS

Extending our respect and love to others . . .
the key to creating unity in the world . . .

The Long-Term Vision: Loving-kindness and Sustainable Villages and Families

There is a teaching story about a visit to heaven and hell:

> The people in hell were emaciated, sitting around a table with gigantic utensils, unable to feed themselves.
>
> In heaven, the people had the same gigantic utensils, but fed each other across the table.

Beyond the *greed and turf war,* competitive and disingenuous economic systems of the last two hundred years, if our world is to heal itself, we need an new economic and social system based on *producing goods or services that really help people and nature.* We need to create a new economic and social system that *values self-love and self-care, love and care for others, and love and care for the environment.*

An example in this new system would be paying a next-door neighbor to check in with someone who has just come home from the hospital. People could accrue *redeemable credits for acts of kindness* in a *community care account.* The sociologist Ruth Benedict said *societies work when virtue pays.*

This *virtue pays system* needs to happen to save the planet. It took 1 million years to get to a population of 1 billion people, but we are now adding a billion people to the planet every ten years. We are now at 6.85 billion and it will be 9 to 11 billion by 2050, depending on whether or not we can create sustainable villages that can provide local work for all residents, which leads to smaller families.

Greed and war are complete anachronisms. Humanity has to consciously transform quickly. We need a commission of creative thinkers to get together, including people such as:

• Hazel Henderson—http://hazelhenderson.com/

Hazel Henderson is the founder of Ethical Markets Media, LLC and the creator and co-executive producer of its television series. She is a world-renowned futurist, evolutionary economist, a worldwide syndicated columnist, a consultant on sustainable development, and author of the Axiom and Nautilus award-winning book *Ethical Markets: Growing the Green Economy* (2006) and eight other books. She co-edited, with Harlan Cleveland and Inge Kaul, *The UN: Policy and Financing Alternatives*, Elsevier Scientific, United Kingdom 1995 (United States edition, 1996).

• David Korten—www.davidkorten.org/

Dr. David C. Korten is an author and an outspoken critic of corporate globalization. He is probably best known as the author of the book *When Corporations Rule the World*. His most recent book is *The Great Turning: From Empire to Earth Community*, which places corporate globalization within the context of 5,000 years of "Empire," used as a generic term for organizing human relationships by dominator hierarchy. Korten argues that the human system has now reached the limits of domination that social and environmental systems will tolerate. To secure its future, the human species must turn away from the dominator way of Empire to the partnership way of Earth Community, as defined by the principles of the Earth Charter.

• Steven Rockefeller

Steven Rockefeller coordinated the drafting of the Earth Charter for the Earth Charter Commission and Earth Council. In 2005 he moderated the International Launch of the United Nations Decade of Education for Sustainable Development (DESD) (2005–2014) in its headquarters in New York, launched by UNESCO and attended by Nane Annan, the wife of Secretary General Kofi Annan. He has a Master of Divinity from the Union Theological Seminary in New York City and a Ph.D. in philosophy of religion from Columbia University. He is currently Professor Emeritus of Religion at Middlebury College in Middlebury, Vermont where he previously served as Dean of the College and chairman of the religion department. Published books include *Spirit and Nature—Why the Environment Is a Religious Issue: An Interfaith Dialogue,* edited by Steven C. Rockefeller and John C. Elder (Beacon Press, 1992).

We are engaged in
'shamanic transformational work'
to save humanity and the planet by creating a
global transformational co-creative network.

Let us continue to join forces and be more
powerfully expressed, creative,
loving, and collaborative each day.

Each of Us Is a Precious Part
of the Human Family

B.K.S. Iyengar, one of the most highly respected yogis alive today, lends inspiration in his comment from his book, *The Tree of Yoga:* "As the essence of the tree is hidden in the seed, so the essence of (the human) is in the seed of the soul." A yoga student of mine said that "this seed is our own unique gift, as different in each of us as a fingerprint. Recognizing our gift and pursuing it passionately is, therefore, a sacred duty . . ."

So, we see that each seed contains the potential of its unique form and place in the world. Without water, light, and soil, the seed's potential remains locked inside. When it receives nourishment from water, light, and soil, its potential awakens and is born into the world, offering flower, fruit, essence, and medicine.

The same is true for humans. Our seed potential lies dormant until just the right environment allows it to blossom and be born into the world. The longer it is locked inside, the more we may forget our true self and our unlimited potential. We may even forget how connected we are to nature itself.

But we find that just as with any seed, the pain of remaining suppressed or closed off in a human family can eventually get so intensely uncomfortable that family members seeking growth will break out from their containment at some point in their lives. Not always; yet often enough. And we go out into the world to find ourselves.

Responsibility, discernment, and discipline must accompany this process of breaking free of the containment of the seed for that growth to be strong and healthy. We must reconnect to the Greater Good and understand how each action, thought, or choice deeply affects the earth and all its creatures—humans, plants, fish, and animals. We are dependent on each other, although some days it seems we are independent. We know now, from seeing recent weather changes, just how connected we are. Past choices have brought us up to this moment—lack of alternative energy sources, job shortages, collapsing economies, obesity, and chronic stress.

In the yoga tradition, there is a story that tells us that the world is woven together in space. This weaving is called Indra's Net. At the intersection of each strand is a jewel. The human soul is this jewel. In this tradition, each human soul has its own teaching or dharma to play out in a lifetime. How we do it will affect every fiber that is part of Indra's Net.

This is where responsibility plays a part. Through ethical, moral, and discerning choices the human soul keeps its part on Indra's Net functioning as a beautiful patchwork. One may have to give something up or change something to keep the holistic approach at the forefront rather than selfish desires. Giving up something might include unhealthy relationships, careers, an old way of thinking, or unhealthy dietary habits.

The jewel of each human soul can be in service to others. This keeps the Human Family together. Every decision, every action can be done for the Greater Good of All rather than for just a brief selfish act without regard for the rest of the jewels on Indra's Net.

Our lives and our gifts are precious gems that can enhance life on Earth for every being, every plant, and every animal—not just for our own personal dramas.

We are here to serve.
We are here to play a part in this thing called Life.
How can I help you today?
What would make your life more wonderful
(little sparrow, sweet petunia, baby rabbit, tiny ant)?

—PAULA TEPEDINO, YOGA TEACHER
AND LOVER OF NATURE

CHAPTER 5

Platonic Altruistic Love

LOVE =
caring about each other's well-being
+ sharing heartfelt experiences with each other
+ working and playing well together
(as they used to say on report cards)

—SANDY HINDEN

PLATONIC LOVE BETWEEN THINKERS AND FOR KNOWLEDGE

A loving heart is the beginning of all knowledge.

—THOMAS CARLYLE

The term platonic love will be used here as the love for ideas, study, and philosophy.

It can also refer to the appreciation a student and a teacher can have in their search for knowledge and understanding and the great appreciation they may have for each other.

We can also use the term platonic love to mean an intimate companionship or relationship, especially between two persons of the opposite sex, characterized by the absence of sexual involvement; and the presence of friendly, intellectual affection. In platonic love we appreciate each other's thinking, values, and ideals. This chapter looks at how love for ideals has led to social improvements through movements and conscious social action designed to transform social, economic, and political systems.

Altruistic Love-in-Action

Loving Transformation is a process of collaboration and dialogue that is built on a history of resisting what is not wanted to create a better situation. In Loving Transformation the *force of conscious, loving creativity* is employed to organize people to create the world, community, workplace, family, or relationship we really want by creating a shared vision, goals, and objectives, and taking committed focused action to achieve agreed-upon objectives within a timetable we establish.

Past methodologies of nonviolent resistance (nonviolent action) to achieve sociopolitical goals through social action are mostly known through Mohandas Gandhi and Martin Luther King, Jr. They used methods of nonviolent passive resistance and noncooperation, and risked arrest. Gandhi's *satyagraha,* "truth force," was developed to search for truth and attempted to change the heart, as well as the actions, of the opponent. Movements promoting philosophies of nonviolence or pacifism have adopted methods of nonviolent action as effective ways to achieve social and political goals. Historically, nonviolent resistance tactics include:

- Vigils
- Community education through information distribution
- Consciousness-raising gatherings
- Protest art, music, and poetry
- Tax resistance

- Refusal to enter war
- Boycotts—refusing to buy products
- Underground railroads
- Picket lines
- Boycotts
- Sanctions
- Legal and diplomatic negotiation
- Public refusal of awards and honors
- Sabotage of weapons
- Marches and rallies
- General strikes
- Rent strikes and work slowdowns
- Letter writing and petition campaigns
- Bank-ins, property occupancy, and financial withdrawals
- Lobbying
- Political denial through voting
- Political action committees
- Legislative campaigns

Learning from the work of Gandhi, Martin Luther King, Jr. popularized the term "Beloved Community", first expressed in the early twentieth century by the founder of the Fellowship of Reconciliation, Josiah Royce.

Dr. King's Beloved Community is a global vision in which love and trust win out over hatred and fear. Cooperation is nurtured through friendly action. Discrimination and intolerance give way to a spirit of inclusion and appreciation. Personal and international disputes dissolve through commitment to nonviolence, peaceful conflict-resolution, and reconciliation of adversaries.

The cycle of retributive violence gives way to lasting peace through reconciliation and healing. Peace with justice prevails over war and military conflict, and poverty, hunger, and homelessness are ended. The wealth of the earth is shared. This is the vision of the "Beloved Community" envisioned by Josiah Royce and Martin Luther King, Jr. and millions of their followers today.

Dr. King expressed this type of understanding that goodwill would transform negativity into positivity, and love would bring about miracles in the hearts of people. Nonviolence would create the Beloved Community through a new relationship between the oppressed and the oppressor.

Dr. King distinguished between three types of love:

1. **Eros**—aesthetic or romantic love;

2. **Philia**—affection between friends;

3. **Agape, unconditional love**—understanding, redeeming goodwill for all, an overflowing love which is purely spontaneous, unmotivated, groundless, and creative; the love of God operating in the human heart.

Today, the King Center, in Atlanta, Georgia embraces the conviction that the Beloved Community can be achieved through a commitment to nonviolence and the study and practice of six principles and steps of nonviolence that become a way of life. These principles develop relationships that resolve conflict, reconcile adversaries, and advance social, economic, and political improvements in your community and nation.

In the six principles, Dr. King expressed belief that nonviolence is a way of life for courageous people. It seeks to win friends and create understanding; it seeks to defeat injustice, not people; it holds that suffering is educational and transformational; it chooses to love instead of hate; and believes that the universe is on the side of justice—that we are evolving into a just society.

CHOOSE TO LOVE INSTEAD OF HATE

Dr. King taught that no matter what hurtful people do through intimidation, threats, distributing hate literature, attacks, beatings, or bombings, that we wear hurtful people down and win the victory of freedom and justice through our capacity to nonviolently withstand the suffering and not react with hostility and violence, and by being loving. He thought that we could win over the hurtful person through this process by appealing to his or her heart and conscience.

Love-in-Action: 7 Steps to Transform Situations

1. **Realign Your Inner Being to Love.** Methods of transformational love are vibrational, and work with consciousness and energy.

   - Switch from the consciousness of negativity, chaos, and hate to love, recognizing that all life is interrelated.

   - Re-center yourself in self-love, inner peace, happiness, and well-being.

   - Imagine transforming injustice and restoring community.

   - Release specific inner negativity about the hurtful person.

   - Imagine yourself being proactive rather than being passive, cynical, or resigned. Release believing the other person can't or won't change. Be open to the other changing.

   - Be open to unforeseen events happening in the hurtful person's life that may cause an inner shift.

   - Be ceaselessly compassionate and forgiving to restore a sense of community.

   - Be lovingly spontaneous, unselfish, and creative.

2. **Be Open to Understanding.** Gather information and points of view by doing research to increase your understanding of

the issue or problem. Use the Internet, the library, past and present articles, radio, television, and talking to people who have expertise in the issue. Understand the other person's point of view and his or her underlying feelings, values, and needs. Clarify, understand, and formulate a clear sentence describing the injustice or concern facing you or the community.

3. **Be Informative.** Inform others, including the difficult person, about your issue. This minimizes misunderstanding and gains you sympathy and support. Clarify how you can work together to create a better situation. If he or she is adamant and negative, inform others about his or her tactics, bullying, undermining, and lack of integrity and respect.

4. **Bounce Back.** Each day recommit to long-term Love-in-Action. Daily, replace your own cynicism, hatred, resentment, and resignation and reaffirm your love-for-life. Loosen the grip of your ego and become aware of any hidden or selfish motives that you may have of wanting to look good and make the other person look bad, or to punish him or her. That person is your "brother or sister" and you don't want to harm him or her. You want to transform the situation to a better one. Recognize that some changes can happen quickly, some changes take longer, and some take a lifetime. Accept the situation as it is right now. Recognize your suffering with compassion and forgiveness. Continue to work for justice, peace, wellbeing, and abundance for all, aligned with nature.

5. **Create Win-Win Solutions.** Use serenity, patience, humor, and creativity to explore what the other really needs. Go over your list of grievances and concerns and create a plan to address and resolve each item. Creatively look for ways in which the other can also win. Understand the other's feelings, values and real needs. Seek to create "additive solutions" that address all parties' deeper needs.

6. **Take Action to Create Healing.** Create an atmosphere for understanding with the other party. Take actions to have the other party work with you to create solutions that resolve the injustice, grievance, or concern.

7. **Stay Open.** Leave room for further collaboration and creativity to develop that you may not presently imagine could occur. Be open to unforeseen possibilities and opportunities coming into your life. Create a clearing by letting go of all preconceived ideas and attachments to the situation, being open to fresh beginnings.

The Truth Force of Mohandas Karamchand Gandhi— Truth and Love in Action

Martin Luther King, Jr. was greatly influenced by the philosophy of Mohandas Gandhi and his work in Africa and India. Gandhi worked with the principle of *satyagraha*. The word *satya* (truth), is derived from *sat,* which means "being." He believed that nothing is, or exists in reality, except truth. To Gandhi, truth (*satya*) implied love, and firmness (*agraha*) served as a synonym for force. Thus, he began to call the Indian movement *satyagraha*, the force which is born of truth and love or nonviolence. He gave up the use of the phrase *passive resistance* and replaced it with *truth and love force.*

Gandhi's *truth-told-with-love* left a potent legacy to India and the world in the technique of *satyagraha*. In this instrument of truth and love-in-action, there is a power to effect change.

In *satyagraha*, the truth force is willing to endure great personal suffering in order to do what's right. The Sanskrit word comes from the roots of:

1. *Sat*—Truth, openness, honesty, and fairness.

2. *Ahimsa*—Refusal to inflict injury on others.

3. *Tapasya*—Willingness for self-sacrifice.

Code of Discipline

In the 1930s movement, Gandhi created a code of conduct for the volunteers. It included: harboring no anger, but rather absorbing the anger of the opponent and refusing to return the assault of the opponent; not submitting to any order given in anger, even though severe punishment is threatened for disobeying; refraining from insults and swearing; protecting opponents from insult or attack, even at the risk of life; not resisting arrest. If taken prisoner, behaving in an exemplary manner.

Steps in a Satyagraha Campaign

The outline below is applicable to a movement growing out of grievances against an established political order. These steps could be adapted to other conflict situations.

1. Negotiation and arbitration
2. Preparation of the group for direct action
3. Agitation
4. Issuing of an ultimatum
5. Economic boycott and forms of strike
5. Noncooperation
7. Civil disobedience
8. Usurping of the functions of government
9. Parallel government

Gandhi and other Indian leaders accepted everyone who would join their campaigns. They developed tactics and rules as they moved to meet well-advanced situations of conflict. If they had been able to select their group leaders and to train them for their respective roles in the satyagraha operation, the movements might well have been even more dramatic.

BASIC CONCEPTS OF SATYAGRAHA— GANDHIAN NONVIOLENCE

Sat—Truth, openness, honesty, and fairness

- Each person's opinions and beliefs represent part of the truth.

- In order to see more of the truth we must share our truths cooperatively.

- There is a desire to communicate and a determination to do so, which in turn requires developing and refining relevant skills of communication.

- Commitment to seeing as much of the truth as possible means that we can not afford to categorize ourselves or others.

Ahimsa—Refusal to inflict injury on others

- Violence shuts off channels of communication.

- Ahimsa is dictated by our commitment to communication and to sharing our pieces of the truth.

- The concept of *ahimsa* appears in most major religions, which suggests that while it may not yet be practiced by most people, it is respected as an ideal.

- *Ahimsa* is an expression of our concern that our own and other's humanity be manifested and respected.

- We must learn to genuinely love our opponents in order to practice *ahimsa*.

Tapasya—Willingness for self-sacrifice

- A *satyagrahi* (one who practices *satyagraha*) must be willing to shoulder any sacrifice which is occasioned by the struggle they have initiated, rather than pushing such sacrifice or suffering onto their opponents, lest the opponents become alienated and access to their portion of the truth become lost.

- The *satyagrahi* must always provide a face-saving "way out" for the opponents.
- The goal is to discover a wider vista of truth and justice, not to achieve victory over the opponent.

> Violence shuts off channels of communication.
> We must learn to genuinely love our opponents
> in order to practice *ahimsa*.
> The goal is to discover a wider vista of truth and justice,
> not to achieve victory over the opponent.
> Deeply listening from the heart
> is the first half of truth communication.
> Compassionately speaking from the heart
> is the second half of truth communication.

FREEDOM TO ESPOUSE IDEAS OF HATRED OR LOVE IN THE COMMUNITY

In late October 2008, as Barack Obama was about to win the presidential election, the Ku Klux Klan made a move in Suffolk County, New York, leafletting cars at the Deer Park Railroad Station. As a community developer, I sensed this was the beginning of a process that, unless contained, would grow. Fanatics depend on the average person doing nothing. I wrote an e-mail letter calling for a rally, but was then counseled by a good friend, who was a former police trainer and police bodyguard to public figures. He asked me to consider insurance and possible violence that might occur—were we prepared for that? I realized we were not organized enough, and not prepared for the violence that might occur. I decided to request that the "powers that be" hold a press conference condemning harassment and violence by hate groups. It was simpler and less costly in terms of possible confrontation with violent agitators. I sent the following e-mail to eighty people I knew locally, nationally, and globally.

We reserve the right of free speech to state our views whether our enemies like it or not.
The IKA (Imperial Klans of America) hates:
Muds, spics, kikes, and niggers.
—*From the Imperial Klans of America website (www.kkk.net)*

We have seen over and over again, that freedom to speak and spread hatred breeds harassment, intimidation, subjugation, and ultimately violence.
—*www.splcenter.org/news/item.jsp?aid=312*

I say, "Never again will we sit back and be harassed."
—*Sandy Hinden*

The opposite of love is not hate, it's indifference!
—*Elie Wiesel*

All that is needed for evil to triumph
is for good people to do nothing.
—*Edmund Burke*

To Clergy, Nonprofit, Business, and Government Leaders of Nassau and Suffolk County, Long Island:

On Wednesday morning, October 22, 2008, it was reported on National Public Radio that 100 Klu Klux Klan flyers were posted on car windshields at the Deer Park Railroad Station in Suffolk County, Long Island.

It was further reported that Suffolk Country responded saying the KKK had the right to freedom of speech.

We are calling upon you to join forces with us to request Suffolk County Executive Steve Levy, Nassau County Executive Thomas Suozzi, Suffolk County Police Commissioner Richard Dormer, and Nassau County Police Commissioner Lawrence Mulvey hold a joint press conference condemning harassment and violence, and assure the public they will do all they can to protect the public from harassment and violence of hate groups.

We urge you to take a stand and add your name to this request for our County Executives to speak up for Justice, Tolerance and Unity in our communities.

Please add your name, position and organization below and send it to me.

Please distribute this to leaders on Long Island and encourage them to sign on.

Thank you for your courage and commitment to the well-being of all people on Long Island.

Sandy Hinden

A week later, I circulated the proposal found on the following pages.

In November of 2008, one month after the circulation of this e-mail, seven young men in Suffolk County were accused of taunting and punching Marcelo Lucero, thirty-seven, a serious-minded man from Ecuador who had lived in the United States for sixteen years. One of the seven men was accused of stabbing and killing him. All have pleaded not guilty.

In late January 2009, prosecutors believed that many more teenagers were involved in attacks on Hispanics in and around

Three New Strategies for Responding to Local & National Hate Groups

1. Anti-hate, pro-recovery website
2. Countywide security network alert & warnings
3. Rage and bully treatment

Pro-Freedom of Speech Advocate

"We need to remember that words are not actions. People who are sane know the difference. People who think that if you hate someone you should kill them, really, those people need to be stopped, obviously, and either locked up or treated."

Anti-Hate Speech Advocate

"I think people who espouse hate were abused and brainwashed and don't know it . . . 'hurt people often hurt people' . . . I have compassion for them and wish there was a way for them to get treatment . . . but in the meantime, I will do all I can to counteract their hateful speech by warning them they will be arrested if they hurt anyone."

While the constitutionalists debate freedom-to-use-hate-speech, it is time a new set of tools be developed to help those vulnerable to becoming part of hate groups and using hate speech.

WHY: *Organized hate speech is intended to intimidate and subjugate innocent people. In the past, it has influenced some to take action to cause violence.*

In an age of automatic weapons, hate speech can cause massive harm very quickly. Two weeks before the November 2008 presidential election, two young skinheads were arrested for plotting to go into a school and use automatic weapons to shoot and kill eighty-eight black students, behead fourteen more, and then kill Barrack Obama in a drive-by shooting.

It is known that many men were abused in childhood by bullies in the home, school, and community. It is also known by treatment professionals that "hurt people often hurt people." Today's bullies, skinheads, neo-Nazis, and KKK members were often bullied in their childhood and are prone to being abusive today in the home, workplace, and community.

Strategy One: Anti-Hate, Pro-Recovery Web Site

A website needs to be supported by the Justice Department devoted to treating rageaholics and bullies. All forms of hate group bullies need our compassion, understanding, and treatment. They need to have web-based resources to begin to address and heal their hurt, hate, and rage.

Strategy Two: Countywide Security Network Alert and Warnings

When skinheads, KKK, or neo-Nazis leaflet and promote their activities in a community, it is essential to form and activate a Countywide Security Network made up of the County Supervisor, Police Commissioner, and leaders from the clergy, business, education, and health and human services. They should hold a press conference and clearly state that they will do all they can to protect the public and arrest any and all hate promoters involved with harassment and violence.

Strategy Three: Rage and Bully Treatment

A program for treating rageaholics and bullies would include learning to express anger constructively through study and practice of:

- Meditation
- Mediation
- Conflict resolution
- Assertiveness training
- Co-counseling
- Anger release work
- Non-violent (compassionate) communication
- Stephen R. Covey's *The Seven Habits of Highly Effective People: Powerful Lessons in Personal Change*

Patchogue, and are still at large. Investigators believe that there is a separate group of teenagers who roam Patchogue on bicycles attacking Latinos.

In March of 2009, in neighboring Nassau County on Long Island, Darryl Jackson, an elderly black man, was beaten to the ground by four Latino men outside a Roosevelt deli. One of the Hispanic men was a New York City police officer. Witnesses, and the victim, said the attackers used racial slurs. Following the attack, a "Group for Community Unity" formed to seek justice, address underlying social, economic and educational issues causing racial intolerance, and foster understanding between the black and Hispanic communities in Nassau County.

CREATING A CIVILIZATION OF LOVE

We have all seen that returning violence for violence multiplies violence, that hate cannot drive out hate. Only love can do that. Hate eats away at community unity, destroys a person's sense of values, and clouds objectivity. It causes one to perceive the good as bad, and bad as good, confusing the true and the false, and seeing the false as true. Once this confusion takes hold, violence is permissible. We need to help the young reject hatred, revenge, aggression, and retaliation. The basis for doing so is love.

When I was in college, I took a course in utopian societies in the Contemporary Civilization Department. The reading list consisted of:

- *The Republic,* by Plato
- *Utopia,* by Thomas More
- *Looking Backward,* by Edward Bellamy
- *Walden II,* by B.F. Skinner

So—keeping the dream alive for an enlightened society—how can we create a civilization of love when there is so much hatred, addiction, greed, violence, egotism, and individualism all around us?

It has to come about one person at a time, and be supported by a culture and education for loving-kindness.

This is my dream . . . a call for co-creative collaboration . . .

A NEW SYSTEM—LOVING KINDNESS AND SUSTAINABLE VILLAGES AND FAMILIES

There is a teaching story about a visit to heaven and hell that has been mentioned earlier in this book: The people in hell were emaciated, sitting around a table with gigantic utensils, unable to feed themselves. In heaven, the people had the same gigantic utensils, but fed each other across the table.

We need a system based on producing goods or services that really help people and nature.

We need to create a new system that values *self-love and self-care, love and care for others, and love and care for the environment.* An example is paying a next-door neighbor to check in with someone who has just come home from the hospital. People could accrue redeemable credits for acts of kindness in a *community care account,*. The sociologist Ruth Benedict said *societies work when virtue pays.*

This *virtue pays system* needs to happen to save the planet because:

- It took 1 million years to reach 1 billion people on earth in 1800.

- In 2009, we are near 7 billion people on earth.

- We are now adding a billion people to the planet every 10 years.

- We will have 9 to 12 billion people on earth by 2050, depend-

ing on whether or not we can create sustainable villages, that
lead to local work for all, which leads to smaller families.

- Greed and war are anachronisms. Humanity has to consciously transform it economic system quickly.

- By 2050, there will be 4 billion people struggling to survive
and 3 billion people living desperate lives, unless we transform the economic system of the world to support sustainable
communities.

We need to quickly transform humanity and the planet . . .
let us gather with others interested in global transformational cocreation . . . let us join forces and collaborate more
powerfully.

How do we build a "civilization of love"? How do we defeat
the culture of death? How do we confront hatred, neglect, and
egotistical individualism?

As utopian as it may sound, we build a "civilization of love"
by loving one another constantly and intensely. As St. Peter said:

Since you have purified yourselves by obedience
to the truth for sincere mutual love,
love one another intensely
from a (pure) heart.

—1 PETER 1:22

We need to encourage each other daily to help in small ways
to create a "civilization of love." As hatred makes us isolated, it is
through solidarity of love that we can fully participate in life, in
our communities, and calling for transformation nationally and
globally.

We need to give up many things to achieve this. We must:

1. Dissolve past hurts and pain and heal emotionally . . .

LONG ISLAND MEN'S CENTER • MARCH 2009

For Immediate Release

"Sandy Hinden learned much in 30 years of local, national, and community development work that saw him create gardens around the world for children to grow food and friendship, and link 50 peace museums in the world with the United Nations. At a 2005 United Nations Interfaith Conference for Peace, he spoke to 1,500 people . . .

The world will never be at peace unless you create sustainable communities . . . there are 500,000,000 men roaming around the planet looking for work. When men don't have constructive work, they get into trouble selling drugs, guns, and weapons of all kinds. We need a *World Works Program* to help men find a job or they will be drawn into gangs, organized crime, piracy, and now terrorism.

Men need help, guidance, counseling and work to be able to have a decent home and family. We will go from 6.5 billion people on earth in 2005, to somewhere between 9 to12 billion people on the planet by 2050. If we don't help men, they will create more violence, war and terrorism.

When Sandy Hinden came home from the 2005 UN Interfaith Conference for Peace he began to plant the seeds of the Long Island Men's Center. He began reaching out to good men he knew. The Long Island Men's Center has grown to have monthly meetings and an annual retreat.

All men locally, nationally or from around the world are welcome each month and at the Long Island Men's Gathering—LI-MEGA—in October."

2. Empty ourselves and move away from the "I" to recognize "the other" and "we" . . .

3. Give up cynicism, sarcasm, hostility, resentment, resignation, and grudges,,,

4. Release our desire for exploitive sex, money, and power . . .

5. Let go of accumulating money to show off and travel excessively . . . and actively participate in building a sustainable, ecofriendly community where you live . . .

6. Give up excess possessions and things in favor of healthy, loving relationships . . .

7. Recycle much as possible . . .

We need to create a new economic system that values simplicity, self-love, and self-care, love and care for others, and love and care for the environment. We can live simply and lovingly so others may live.

There are two kinds of power: power obtained through fear of punishment and energy gained through acts of love. Power based on hatred and punishment is short-lived and offensive, while power based on love is effective, permanent, and joyful. Cowards are incapable of expressing love. Expressing love is a power possessed by the brave of heart. Powerfully refuse to accept the view that humanity is tragically bound to the present system of hostility, ego, and consumption to be happy. Peace and love can become a reality through believing in the powerful truth and guiding star that unconditional love will have the final word on planet Earth.

Modern economists measure the "standard of living" by the amount of annual consumption, assuming that we need to consume more to live a better life. In the civilization of love, with its *care and love economy*, consumption is not a means to well-being.

In a care and love economy we love and take care of ourselves, each other, and the environment, and obtain the maximum potential of well-being with the minimum of consumption. With less toil devoted to the cycle of consuming junk media/feeling inner pain/using addictions to numb the pain/obsession to earn more and more/shopping to numb the pain/disposing of stuff to make way for more stuff, there is more time and energy left for participating in community sustainability projects and artistic and creative expression.

While modern economics considers consumption to be the sole end and purpose of all economic activity, the economics of care and love deals with the real life problems we all face: caring for the young, the old, ourselves, and the environment. Wealth in the new economy of care and love means well-being. Greed and envy demand continuous and limitless economic growth and use of resources. This kind of material growth, unlike spiritual growth, has little regard for conservation and cannot possibly fit into a finite environment. We must therefore give up the essential nature of greedy capitalism and rapidly develop the possibility of evolving an alternative system that will heal people and the planet. We must shift from an industrial growth society to a life-sustaining civilization based on care and love.

The ecological and social crises we face have been created by an economic system based on accelerating growth and ever-expanding consumption. This creates a self-destructing political economy.

When we set goals and measure performance on how quickly materials can be extracted from the earth, turned into consumer products and used to produce weapons—with little concern for consumer waste and all for the purpose of ever-increasing profits—we are on a collision course with the environment and society's ability to care for its people.

We are in the midst of a *revolution of the heart*, as people realize that our needs can be met without destroying our world. Once there is conviction and commitment of the heart we can use our imagination, technical know how, communication systems, and resources to grow enough food, ensure clean air and water, meet energy needs, and create health care in loving, sustainable ways.

As millions of individuals all around the world awaken from a deep consumer trance to the reality of our global crisis we can act out of love, compassion, and a deep sense of responsibility to people and planet. The future is a matter of choice, co-creativity, and co-empowerment—a new business model of win-win-win. I win, you win, the community and nature wins.

Tips for Transformation to a Caring and Loving Economy

- ❥ Boycott junk food, junk media and junk relationships . . .
- ❥ Refuse to be disempowered by media, others responses, or your own thinking . . .
- ❥ Bounce back from setbacks and do not turn to shopping to alleviate pain . . .
- ❥ End your addictions through daily compassion and forgiveness for yourself and others . . .
- ❥ Give up memories of the past that disempower you . . .
- ❥ Tell your heart today is the best day of your life . . . let your heart sing its joy . . .
- ❥ Have inner-love, appreciation and respect for yourself, no matter what happens . . . appreciate others and life . . .
- ❥ Take action to enjoy yourself with healthy pleasures in the present . . .
- ❥ Take action to create an abundant future based on wellbeing, healthy-loving relationships, and sustainable communities . . .

As we take personal action to create a personal life of caring and loving we are creating our own economy of caring and loving, and a civilization of love for every person, the planet, and life as a whole.

CONVICTION AND COMMITMENT OF THE HEART

Take time each day, even for only ten minutes in the morning or evening, to meditate to be serene and loving within your self. Once you have peace, love, joy, compassion and forgiveness inside yourself to tap into each day, you will be unstoppable in your ability to transform suffering in difficult situations by contributing your peace and serenity. The most important thing is for you to have freedom—the ability to *shift* your thinking; *stability*—the ability to tap into balance and harmony; and *peace*—the ability to re-center yourself with acceptance and serenity in your heart. Then you will help relieve the suffering around you, turning chaos into balance and harmony.

Train yourself to love properly to be able to give happiness and joy each day. Practice *deeply looking* at the person you love. Love comes from understanding. As you understand this person, your love will deepen. Peace and love are won by those who give up their rigid positions of being right and making the other person wrong, and giving up looking good and making the other look bad. Love comes from opening your mind and heart to seek out *connection* and *deeper understanding*.

In addition to understanding, love also requires commitment, empathy, integrity, and authenticity to grow. You must be real for love to grow. You need to give up pretending and concealing the truth and share truthfully what is going on for you. Become integral—one with your self. Aligning the parts inside yourself so there is congruency. Create a conviction to tell the truth, with compassion.

Remember Gandhi's *satyagraha,* his loving-truth-force, and its willingness to endure great personal suffering in order to do what is right.

Sat

- Truth, openness, honesty, and fairness.
- Share what is real for you . . .
- Be authentic . . .
- Keep your word, let others know when you don't . . .
- And recommit to doing so . . .

Ahimsa

- Refusal to inflict injury on others. . . .
- Let go of hostility, resentment, and grudges . . .
- Share what is happening with compassion and forgiveness . . .

Tapasya

- Willingness for self-sacrifice . . .
- Be willing to give up your egotistical position . . .
- Give up being right and looking good . . .
- Stop making others wrong and making them look bad . . .
- Let go of your attachment to power and control . . .
- Be open minded . . .

Be an embodiment of truth and love.
Love, honor, and cherish your self.
Love, honor, and cherish others.
Love, honor, and cherish the earth.
This way you are actively creating
the Civilization of Love each day.

A MANIFESTO FOR A CIVILIZATION
OF TRUTH, WISDOM, AND LOVE

You have the power to take charge of your life and stop being dependent on people, places, substances, or things for your love, self-esteem, and wellbeing. As you awaken to the healing wisdom within, you become authentic and trust the healing power of the truth. Powerfully face what beliefs, addictions, and dependent behavior were created by the people and culture around you that you absorbed and now don't need. Become clear on those things inside you that you may feel inferior about, ashamed of, or guilty for having done. Release them and give them up as not real. Affirm and enjoy your self, your truth, heartfulness, compassion, creativity, and wisdom. Stop pretending you are not incredibly wonderful. Stop hiding your truth, heartfulness, compassion, creativity, and wisdom. You are a great human being. Let go of all thoughts and feelings of blame, shame, or guilt, and any behavior that keeps you from fully loving and expressing yourself. Get completion on the past by making a list of people you may have intentionally or unintentionally hurt or were hurt by. Clear out any negative energy by apologizing and committing to changing your behavior to not do that again. Share your grievances in a respectful way. Trust your reality and affirm that what you see, know and feel is important. Also, know that what you see, know, and feel is inside of you. Trust yourself and be open to respectfully learning about the other person's interior life. Promptly admit your current mistakes and breaches of integrity when you failed to honor your word or not do what you said you would do. Make amends when appropriate, only when it will not cause harm to others. Never say you are sorry for things you did not do, cover up for or take responsibility for the shortcomings of others. Don't become mentally caught up in analyzing others; keep the focus on improving your life and mind your own business. Stop trying to fix, change, or control others. Let go of situations and people who are hurtful, harmful, belittling, or demeaning. Continue to seek out situations, work, projects, and people who affirm your heartfulness, compassion, creativity, and wisdom. Take the next best steps to heal and strengthen your physical body, organize your life, reduce stress, and have healthy fun. Find your inner calling and develop the will and wisdom to follow it. Accept what is. Don't pine over the world as you think it should be. Do things to make your community more livable and sustainable. Support making villages sustainable worldwide. Accept the ups and downs of life as natural events you can use as lessons for your growth. Bounce back from failure by bearing defeat without losing heart. Be serenely courageous and assertively proactive all the time. Be unstoppable. Never let other put you down; report abuses. Never let the drama and antics of others create chaos, disruption, and mayhem that become dazzling distractions. Never lose your focus on your gifts and talents. Share your gifts and talents with your community. Focus each day on your MIG—your Most Important Goal—and get it done. Grow in awareness that you are interrelated with all living things. See clearly that life is a blessing. Make your everyday life a sacred expression, aligned with the creation and creative forces in the universe, earth, and people. Motivate the young, all adults, and elders you meet to contribute to restoring peace and balance on planet Earth so we may create a civilization of truth, wisdom and love on earth—paradise—here on earth.

The kind of spirituality we need is one in which people get great joy out of participating in the community to make it sustainable. Not just praying or meditating, although prayer and meditation are definitely valuable. Not only doing yoga, although yoga can be very healthy for you. It is essential for humanity and the earth that people apply the spiritual energy and conscious-

> ### From the Consumption Economy to the Relationship Economy
>
> The economy of the future will not be based on *consumption*, but rather on our *relationships* to ourselves, each other, and nature . . .
>
> It will include the creative, transformational sustainability of new technologies, recycling, and also the full liberation, full expression, grace, and artistry of our caring, loving, joyful, and creative self . . .
>
> —SANDY HINDEN

ness produced from prayer, meditation, or yoga to creating sustainable communities and a sustainable world in balance with nature. Spiritual engagement in the community is a key.

We are stewards of the planet and can be passionate about the earth. We need to collaborate with each other in a great turning away from consumption and possession to the greatest social transformation ever known, the creation of a civilization of conscious truth, caring, loving, and wisdom. Each of us needs to discover the great creative treasure that lies within us, and find expression of those gift and talents now to benefit and heal our lovely Earth . . . one of the most beautiful planets in the universe.

Together we need to build the human and social transformations needed to deeply heal ourselves, each other, and the earth.

The greatest expression on earth is love.

Robert Muller: Saving the Earth

I first met Robert Muller in 1979. He was an Assistant Secretary-General of the UN, and one of the most brilliant and creative people the earth has ever known. You can learn more about him at these websites:

- Robert Muller's 5,000 Plus Idea Dreams for a Better World— www.robertmuller.org

- Good Morning World—www.goodmorningworld.org

- Paradise Earth—www.ParadiseEarth.us

Robert and I shared a love for those values and ideals of humanity that would help us evolve in consciousness to save the planet. We became good friends and creative supporters of each other's work. We share platonic love for each other and for these ideals.

Robert Muller's Idea Dream 116 of 5,000 Ideas

Humanity is not an evolutionary aberration.

Humanity is an evolutionary miracle on a miraculous planet in a tremendous universe.

Our twenty-first century and third millennium agenda must therefore be:

 To help the success of humanity as the most advanced form of evolution;

 To ensure the fulfillment of each miraculous human life, from birth to death;

 To save, reserve, and enhance the miraculous nature and beauty of our biosphere and planetary home.

> We have not always understood well what will be the fate and future of this wonderful (planet Earth) . . .
>
> If we make the wrong decisions, it will be nearly impossible to repair the eroding health and dwindling resources of our precious planet.
>
> The next few years are of utmost importance—we must act with urgency, vision, and audacity.
>
> Each of us must examine our habits of consumption and embrace the challenge of restoring Earth's precious live-giving balance.

Spirituality, World Peace, and Sustained Living

Dr. Diane M. Rousseau is a professional designer and artist, international speaker and writer on higher consciousness, spiritual science and inter-religious understanding for peace and President of the Institute of Spiritual Sciences in Kent, Washington. At Dr. S. L. Gandhi's international Conference on "Economics of Non-violence and the Vision for a Sustainable World," December, 2005 in New Delhi, India, Diane presented a paper on "Spirituality, World Peace and Sustained Living" as guest speaker from the United States. I first met her through Edward Winchester, founder of the Pentagon Meditation Club. Diane is one of the most loving people in the world. She and I have exchanged correspondence about what we think is the inner source of greed. It is caused by a feeling of emptiness within; people try to fill the emptiness within with more money and possessions. What is needed is self-love, self-worth and self-appreciation to heal the heart, which will then naturally create a sustainable world based on nonviolence and compassion.

Dr. S.L. Gandhi is an exponent of the philosophy of ahimsa

and anuvrat (small vow). He is President of Anuvrat Global Organization (Anuvibha), a transnational center devoted to peace and nonviolent action associated with the United Nations Department of Public Information. He has been speaking around the world for many years and spoke as a panel member at the Interactive Hearing with Civil Society held on the eve of the High-Level Dialogue on Interreligious Understanding and Cooperation that took place at the United Nations on Oct. 4–5, 2007.

Dr. S.L. Gandhi wrote this about Diane in November 2007:

It fills my heart with a sense of exhilaration as I write these lines commending the spirit of selfless dedication as evinced by Dr. Diane M. Rousseau, President of the Institute for Spiritual Sciences during my meetings with her in recent years. I have had many opportunities to exchange views with her on the divine message enshrined in the Vedas, Upanishads, the Gita and the sacred lore and I have no hesitation to say that her deep insights have left an indelible impression on my mind. I haven't come across a woman endowed with such rich ancient wisdom and elevated spirituality as Dr. Diane M. Rousseau in the west in the course of my several visits to these countries. She has in her an inexhaustible fund of compassion and love which she exudes wherever she goes. She first came to my conference on Economics of Nonviolence in 2005 held at Delhi and endeared herself to all who came into contact with her. Her presence at an IOU conference and at a dialogue on Science and Spirituality held at Jaipur in 2006 was a source of inspiration to many. In view of her quest for ancient knowledge and her spiritual pursuits, I have decided to work together with her on some projects aimed at popularizing a culture of ahimsa in the west . . .

—Dr. S. L. Gandhi
President, Anuvrat Global Organization

The following are excerpts from Diane Rousseau's speech, followed by her painting of the Divine Mother Lakshmi and a description of her attributes.

The essential purpose of each religion and faith is to be a way to show higher knowledge with human interpretation as inspired from the Divine Intelligence within. It has been proven that higher consciousness brings in the understanding and compassion that each individual is valuable and can contribute to the welfare of all in their own unique way. It is an internal lack in one self, which contributes to apathy toward one's fellow man, and nature in all of its forms . . .

What is not natural is the misnomer that one is unworthy. This idea of unworthiness can be due to past events; other peoples' expressed impressions or treatment of you, your own feelings of lack of self worth.

One must live life in unity from the Light of God within and Divine love within the heart, this is union or yoga. It is not enough to talk of this 'unified field' of all possibilities; we must live it and BE it.

The development, growth, and greater potential of each individual must be recognized. As long as one does not value themselves or see their own potential, they will not value anyone or anything outside of themselves and will be unaware of the unlimited potential that dwells within each person.

As long as one does not understand their own value, they will grasp at material things, have addictions, and misuse others. Material things do not cause violence. What does cause violence and destructive thoughts is jealousy due to one's own lack of self-appreciation . . .

Non-violence is a product of inner peace and unity. One who experiences this inner peace will reflect this in all areas of life and share in life from this understanding.

With meditation it becomes natural; from within, the thoughts are becoming more refined, more compassionate and more attuned with the Universal or Divine Laws. The essence of meditation is to experience peace and this sublime bliss carries over in one's daily life. Non-violence (Ahimsa) can be sustained by the regular practice of meditation combined with higher education for all ages.

The children of today will be your leaders in the future; they must have role models. The values of life must be presented to them . . . The practice of meditation should begin at an early age.

For adults, the practice of meditation leads to better decisions, better living, and better ways of taking care of one's life. The global economy will naturally improve with meditation due to higher states of consciousness along with the natural unfoldment of the unlimited potential within.

The experience of higher consciousness establishes the basis for maintaining peace within oneself, which creates peace naturally in one's environment. From this level of higher consciousness . . . the spiritual understanding shows the interconnected value of all life which creates and sustains unity. Through this integration, the individual has a greater sense of responsibility; this effects the environment and maintains non-violence through the appreciation of the inner and outer values of life. The combination of meditation, spirituality, and education will provide the foundation for even greater economic potentials through the individual's comprehension of obligations to family, society, and government. Spiritually, the individual feels a sense of belonging to humankind through the direct experience of "Oneness" within; crossing boundaries of prejudice and creating harmony in one's family, community, nation, and extending into a global view of unity.

You cannot have an economically sustained society without the personal experience of inner peace. Higher intelligence and the experience of peace within give a self-referral understanding of non-violence, promoting personal productivity in all areas of life. Compassion combined with understanding of the spiritual teachings will reveal through direct experience the greater values for all life.

In July of 2005, I received an email article from a Physicist friend entitled: "Maslow Predicted the Shift." (Author Unknown):

"Abraham Maslow (1908–1970) was a psychologist who became famous for his hierarchy of human needs. In the 1950s, he predicted the transformation of humanity into a realm of spiritual transcendence, but he had no idea just how soon this would develop into a major movement."

The proof of the value of this "vision" is the fact that all of you have come to this Conference for Spirituality and Sustained Economic Living. This is further proof that the "transformation" has already started. Each person has brought their own "vision" for a reality that has its roots in higher values of life. Each person at this conference desires to uplift and restore a better means for all humanity to live in a peaceful sustained world.

Non-violence is a product of higher consciousness due to a cultured heart and increased intelligence. Non-violence means to not harm and this means respecting all life; the way we treat one another, the way we treat animals, the compassion we extend to other life forms and our own selves . . .

We can create a better today and tomorrow; for true and lasting peace on earth begins with each individual.

Through the daily practice of meditation, one gains the highest knowledge. The heart becomes pure and the mind unfolds creating an unlimited potential for receiving and retaining education in any field of learning.

All that is needed to realize a better reality of life is to raise consciousness, restore traditions of respect to establish higher values in all areas of life. This is up to each individual and is a loving obligation for having the gift of life.

We can create peace; we can respect differences and create unity and be the Divine Spark that becomes the Living Flame. Like the Sun, "Surya", we are a part of a Greater Light and can shine our Light which carries love, energy and intelligence for profound understanding and greater appreciation for all life, touching each person, reaching each country and encircling the globe, lifting up all with this peaceful Light of God for an ecological, economically and spiritually sustainable world.

—Diane M. Rousseau

Sri Sri Maha Lakshmi Ma

Sri Sri Maha Lakshmi Ma
Watercolor by Diane M. Rousseau, December 2001 © DMR
Art and Text copyright © 2005 Diane M. Rousseau

*Divine Mother's form rests
in the Eternal Lotus of the cosmos
as Divine Wisdom and Love.*

*She has four arms
signifying the different ways in which
Love, Grace, Beauty, and Divine Supreme Bliss can give.*

*The top left hand is
'Supreme Wisdom and Intelligence'*

*The top right hand is
Supreme Bliss 'Divine Energy' as creativity in action*

*The lower left hand
showers compassion, protection, eternal bliss, and success,
and endeavors to strengthen discipline and the love for
success on all levels of Being*

*The lower right hand
grants love, abundance, and prosperity,
showering all gifts to sustain Spiritual fulfillment,
support all life, and strengthen love*

*May you be ever victorious on all levels of Being,
strength, protection, perseverance, prosperity, and love,
and in all areas of Spiritual life.*

—DIANE M. ROUSSEAU

Transformation of the World
through Love and Nonviolence
Dr. S.L. Gandhi

Love and nonviolence are the eternal values that have in them infinite power to change the world. Some people think that they can change the world to suit their purpose by force, by violence and hatred. The basis of violence is fear. The basis of love is fearlessness. Love and nonviolence rid the people of fear and give rise to a state of happiness in their hearts. Love and nonviolence are synonymous. One whose heart overflows with love can never be violent. Love and nonviolence ensure perpetual peace, which in turn brings happiness and prosperity to humanity. Nonviolence seeks peace through a change of heart. If a change occurs out of fear, respite caused by it is temporary. If a change of heart occurs out of affection and ahimsa, it brings with it permanent peace. Violence and hatred cause death while love and nonviolence give us life and joy.

Jains believe that the world is filled with both good and bad atoms. Love and nonviolence attract auspicious atoms, which act as a shield against terror and violence. It was the power of the auspicious atoms unleashed by Lord Buddha that disarmed the dreaded terrorist Angulimar. When the most dreadful and poisonous snake bit Lord Mahavira the auspicious atoms released by Mahavira's power of ahimsa calmed the snake's fury and transformed it into a venomless peaceful creature. Mahatma Gandhi's ahimsa drove the mighty Britishers away. It is through training in nonviolence that man's violent nature can be changed. We have to expose children to an environment of love and ahimsa, and they will imbibe the spirit of love naturally. Our survival into the third millennium will depend on our ability to generate peaceful atoms through mass campaigns of nonviolence training, which may usher in an era of peace and happiness on this planet.

CHAPTER 6

Creative Love

*Let the beauty of what you love
be what you do.*

—RUMI

Someone or somehow, the universe was created . . . every-thing in the universe was created . . . brought into exis-tence . . . *God created the heaven and the earth* (Genesis 1:1) . . . Everything is caused or grown, produced, or brought about by a course of action or behavior . . . we can consciously produce through imaginative skill and design . . . bringing new life into existence, creating something new . . . when we consciously cre-ate we feel alive, we are in love, in the state of love with what we are creating. Life can get boring and be tiresome when we work hard at something that is not joyful. Creating and discovery opens us up to what is new. What is new is fresh and its creation radiates energy in us.

Creating can be a magical act . . . an act in which you are in love with what you are creating.

Some of us create chaos and destruction in this world . . . these are people who have chaos and destruction inside them . . .

Others among us create with joy inside them, from the love that they feel inside . . . they create love all around them in their part of the world . . .

LOVE FOR CREATIVE WRITING, MUSIC, DANCE, ART, DESIGN, ARCHITECTURE, AND CRAFTS

*We live in a wonderful world
that is full of beauty, charm and adventure.
There is no end to the adventures that we can have
if only we seek them with our eyes open.*

—JAWAHARLAL NEHRU

Music is love in search of a word.

—SIDNEY LANIER

*Life in abundance
comes only through
great love.*

—ELBERT HUBBARD

*. . . and all knowledge is vain save when there is work,
and all work is empty save when there is love; and when
you work with love, you bind yourself, and to one another
and to God. And what is it to work with love? It is to weave
the cloth with threads drawn from your heart, even as if your
beloved were to wear that cloth. It is to build a house with
affection even as if your beloved were to dwell in that house.
It is to sow seeds with tenderness and reap the harvest
with joy even as if your beloved were to eat the fruit . . .
Work is love made visible.*

—KAHILIL GIBRAN

When we work with love in our hearts we are like what we think God is like. Jesus discovered that the *kingdom of heaven*—the kingdom of God, the kingdom of love—is inside us . . . the treasure of heaven-God-love is inside each of us, waiting to be discovered.

How few of us live each day in the kingdom of heaven-God-love. We are easily drawn out of the inner center of goodness-love into the spinning world of chaos and drama that people create from their intense stories, though scintillating advertisements, in powerfully crafted sound bites from the communications experts for politicians, and by the urgencies of the day.

To work with and create with love is to be a co-creator in the kingdom of heaven within.

> *Neither a lofty degree of intelligence nor imagination*
> *nor both together go to the making of genius.*
> *Love, love, love, that is the soul of genius.*
>
> —WOLFGANG AMADEUS MOZART

Where would we be as a civilization if the geniuses who created with love had never existed? Creative love loves the arts, and creates with love around the whole world. Love and creativity have no boundaries in time or space. For the artist in love with life there are no time and space boundaries.

> *The love of one's country is a splendid thing.*
> *But why should love stop at the border?*
>
> —PABLO CASALS

The ancient Greeks had two words for time, *chronos* and *kairos*. *Chronos* refers to chronological or sequential time, while *kairos* signifies a time in between, a moment of undetermined period of time in which something special happens. In *kairos,* time stretches, boundaries disappear, fantasy is evoked, the power of imagination is activated . . . a portal to new dimension opens invisibly . . . the artist enters . . .

While *chronos* is quantitative, *kairos* has a qualitative nature. The artist uses *kairos* to enter a dimension in which *chronos* is transcended. One pass into a timeless and boundless dimension and plays with words, forms, colors, notes, harmonies to create that which is new, not seen before, not heard before, the very special, illuminating, harmonizing, uplifting, healing, nourishing . . .

When we transcend our self-consciousness and our environment, and feel in harmony with something else, be it inspiring music, a colorful sunset, an animal, or another person, what we are becoming attuned with is our inner being in *kairos* . . . in the timeless and boundless heart . . . in the kingdom of heaven-Godlove. We feel more peaceful and relaxed, and in this calm state we act more appropriately, speak more effectively, perform more creatively, and touch, move, and inspire more lovingly.

I think music in itself is healing.
It's an . . . expression of humanity.
It's something we are all touched by.
No matter what culture we're from,
everyone loves music.
—BILLY JOEL

The creative process is . . .
instinct, skill, culture, and a highly creative feverishness . . .
it is a particular state when everything happens very quickly,
a mixture of consciousness and unconsciousness,
of fear and pleasure;
it's a little like making love, the physical act of love.
—FRANCIS BACON

People love mystery,
and that is why they love my paintings.

—SALVADOR DALI

Throughout the time
in which I am working on a canvas
I can feel how I am beginning to love it,
with that love which is born
of slow comprehension.

—JOAN MIRO

Working on our own consciousness is the
most important thing that we are doing at any moment,
and being love is a supreme creative act.

—RAM DASS

The Hurt, Damaged Heart

- It is a cold and cruel world . . .
- People are cold, cruel, and competitive . . .

The Wondering, Seeking Heart

- How did this happen?
- Why did this happen to me?

The Intentionally Healing Heart

- I know life can be better for me and the world . . .

The Forgiving, Compassionate Heart

- I forgive the people who harmed me and life for being difficult at times . . . .
- I have compassion for myself and them . . . they were also abused . . .

- I release the past . . .
- I surrender to healing and a better way of life in balance with nature, creation (God) and higher consciousness . . .

The Peaceful Joyful, Loving, Creative Heart
- I live a life of peace, serenity, balance, harmony, happiness, joy, love, creativity and abundance . . .

We are shaped and fashioned by what we love.

—Goethe

I tell you, the more I think, the more I feel that there is nothing more truly artistic than to love people.

—Vincent van Gogh

The Love of Music

Steven Kroon has been a professional musician for more than thirty-five years. He was born and lived in Harlem until the age of nine. From there he moved to St. Albans, a residential neighborhood in the New York City borough of Queens.

"The year was 1957. My experience of being raised in Queens was very influential. At the time, there were many great jazz and R&B artists living right in our neighborhood. At home, I mostly listened to my father's records, which were Tito Puente, Tito Rodriguez, and Machito. Then, when I would visit my friends, I would listen to all the great jazz artists. Right in my neighborhood were Lester Young, Eddie "Lockjaw" Davis, Count Basie, and many more. Also a great influence on me was the great producer Henry Glover, who lived right on my corner. With all that diversity and style, I would say most of my musical appreciation began with those early years. At this early stage, I progressed to playing percussion. My brother Bobby and I would practice along with the recordings of these great artists, then, as I progressed, I undertook studying with various music teachers. A great influence on me was the great Tommy Lopez, Sr. I took conga lessons with him for quite some time; shortly after that I studied with the great percussionist Dom Um Romäo.

As my career progressed, I began working with such notables as Luther Vandross (1981–2001). I've appeared on seven platinum albums and fifteen world tours, which include two live video performances. Also, an array of television shows from the Tonight Show with Jay Leno to David Letterman, as well as the Grammys. I've also performed with Ron Carter (1987–2004), which included extensive tours of the U.S., Japan, and Brazil, as well as the well-known New York jazz scene. Some of the places we've performed include the Village Vanguard, The Iridium, and The Blue Note chain from the U.S. to Japan. I've also recorded with much of the "Who's Who" in the recording business: names such as Ron Carter, Roberta Flack, Luther Van Dross, Bill Cosby, Aretha Franklin, and Diana Krall, just to name a few.

For the last five years, I've been working on my own solo career, which includes having released two CDs under my own name. The first one is "In My Path," and the second is entitled "Señor Kroon," both of which will be reissued under my own label Kroonatune Records, LLC. I just recently finished my third CD, which is entitled "El Mas Alla" (Beyond), which is distributed by City Hall Records. At this point in my life, I have chosen to devote my time and creativity to pursue my own career. And as always, "On The One."

The Steven Kroon Sextet is high-energy electrifying Jazz with the blend of Afro Cuban and Brazilian music. The Kroon sound is the heartbeat, the rhythm of existence . . . the feeling he captures is the old nostalgic Harlem Latin Jazz sounds from back in the day, with a modern twist.

—FELIPE LUCIANO, MOTIVATIONAL SPEAKER AND WRITER ON THE
   HISTORY OF SPANISH HARLEM (FROM THE CD LINER NOTES)

Steven Kroon is an amazing percussionist whose outstanding musicianship and fantastic stage presence make him heir to the legendary Latin Jazz Bandleaders Tito Puente and Ray Barretto. Kroon is a great crowd pleaser for dancers and serious listeners alike . . .

—JACK KLEINSINGER, *HIGHLIGHTS IN JAZZ,* MUSIC PROMOTER
   (FROM THE CD LINER NOTES)

Why I Love Music

Music has, and always will be my anchor to life. Through music I have been able to evolve into the artist I am today. Music is like a diamond, its multi-faceted form exposing your mind to so many different ideas and colors. What I love about music from my beginnings is what I still love about it now. My first attraction was to the rhythm. The feeling of being hypnotized by the beat. Then, as that got my attention, I was able to focus on the melody, which told the story.

And as I grew more and more involved, I became enchanted with the melodies and chord changes. To be able to create your own music is like the gift of birth, your creation to share with the universe. It's like your first love, all the special nuances one feels that attracts and lures you into its web of creativity. Then before you know it, it's turned into a relationship, and just like any relationship, it requires dedication. You start to practice just to learn how to embrace your instrument.

As you learn how to embrace your instrument, then you practice to learn to love your instrument. Through the practice and devotion comes your own sound and touch. This then exposes you to another level, the feeling of self-expression through your own instrument. This has to be one of the most euphoric feelings in the world. That is why when one performs at a concert, after the show the people in the audience want to talk to you—because you made a connection with them and you touched their soul. Music is a spiritual connection; it brings people together to experience love, happiness, and joy. To know that through my music I'm helping to enlighten and bring some peace to this world is what music has taught me about love.

—STEVEN KROON, PERCUSSIONIST AND BAND LEADER, STEVEN KROON SEXTET (www.stevekroon.com)

LOVE, CREATIVITY, IMAGINATION, INNOVATION, AND INVENTION

Love and imagination often play a part in each other:

- Without positive imagination it is hard to love someone. You can't imagine being with them, caring for then, supporting them, assisting them.

- Imagination and fantasy can conjure up images that fuel the emotions and release hormones, stimulating the body.

- Imagination can create active and addictive fantasy, conjuring up images of sexy others while making love to one's partner. As stimulating as this can be, it can disconnect you from your partner, which is felt, and further disconnect each of you, leading to separation and isolation.

- Imagination is used to understand a prospective love partner by assessing the quality of their character and trustworthiness.

The Power of Imagination to Bring Love to Planet Earth

The source of all creativity is imagination.

One day, I had the most amazing insight about imagination. Here is what I thought:

> The most powerful force in the universe is imagination . . .
> Everything that humans think, create, and do comes from their imagination . . .
> We make up ideas, emotions, and things . . .
> At a certain point in thinking, we can come across the idea that imagination is super powerful and can transport us anywhere in the realm or dimension of imagination . . .
> We can use our imagination to travel to a place at the center of the universe called the Universal Council . . .
> Wherever there are conscious, thinking beings with imagination, in any place in the universe, they can travel in their imaginations to the Universal Council at the Center of the Universe . . .
> There, they can communicate with other beings from all parts of the Universe in *imagination* . . . it is like a super Second Life of the universe . . . (Second Life is a free, 3-D, Internet virtual world where users can socialize, connect, and create a world solely from their imagination, using voice, graphics, and text chat.)
> So, I presented my assessment of life on planet Earth to the representatives from all parts of the universe in the Universal Council . . .
> We can gain wisdom from these *inter-imaginary beings in the Universal Council by asking questions and listening for answers.* . . . I will ask them this question:
>
> How can we bring more love to planet Earth?

The answers: (1) Be at peace; (2) Complete this book; (3) Love.

Albert Einstein knew the vast power of the imagination. This is what he said:

Imagination is more important than knowledge.
For knowledge is limited to all we now
know and understand,
while imagination embraces the entire world,
and all there ever will be to know and understand.

Learn from yesterday,
live for today,
hope for tomorrow.
The important thing is not to stop questioning.

We can't solve problems
by using the same kind of thinking
we used when we created them.

In the middle of difficulty
lies opportunity.

Logic will get you from A to B.
Imagination will take you everywhere.

Imagination is everything.
It is the preview of life's coming attractions.

The true sign of intelligence
is not knowledge, but imagination.

There are two ways to live:
you can live as if nothing is a miracle;
you can live as if everything is a miracle.

Moving Energy in the Body to Be More Creative

Study nature, love nature,
stay close to nature.
It will never fail you.

—FRANK LLOYD WRIGHT

The theory of subtle energy centers of consciousness in the body, called chakras, believes there are seven locations in the body that act as accumulators, generators, or distributors of different permutations of life energy. The seven subtle energy-consciousness states are as follows.

CHAKRA	LOCATION	FUNCTIONS
7. Crown	Top of the head	Transcendence, understanding, bliss, universal oneness
6. Third Eye	Forehead	Intuition, insight
5. Throat	Neck	Communication, creativity
4. Heart	Center of the chest	Nurturing, compassionate, forgiving
3. Solar Plexus	Above the navel area	Will, power, anger or calming emotions, laughter, joy
2. Navel/Sacral	Lower abdomen, genitals	Desire, sexuality, pleasure, procreation, physical power
1. Root/Support	Base of the spine	Gives energy to the physical body, controls fear, increases overall health and helps in grounding

For people who are not in relationships or are just starting relationships, and/or for the disabled who would have a difficult time being sexual, it can be very pleasurable and revitalizing to move energy from sexual zones to the heart, communication, creative, intuitive, and transcendent experiences.

When starting a relationship you need to not be controlled by powerful sexual feelings and thinking. Give yourself time to explore each other emotionally, intellectually, creatively, and socially before you get powerfully involved in sexual energy. Exploring your creative love can be joyous and abundantly rewarding.

Energy Is Energy

Where energy is centered determines what kind it is. If it is centered in your thinking brain, then you are in the *thinking, logical mind*. If it is centered in your heart, you are *feeling love and compassion*. If it is centered in your second chakra/pelvic region, it is *sexual energy for merging and procreation*. The words define the location. Sexual indicates the second chakra; compassion indicates the fourth chakra; feeling the unity of life, nature, and so on indicates the seventh chakra.

Energy cannot be destroyed or produced by itself, but it can be transformed and often is. It can be expressed in terms of light, physics, heat, and sound. In yoga, you can learn how to practice this *law of energy conservation* by moderating all things. You can learn how to moderate desire, power, sleep, and energy in general. There are specific methodologies that are given to help do this easily, and with consistent, steady practice, one can effortlessly become a master of energy conservation. Meditation stands out as being the most effective way to conserve and channel energy.

Of all the earthly music,
that which reaches farthest into heaven
is the beating of a truly loving heart.
—HENRY WARD BEECHER

A CREATIVE BREAKTHROUGH ABOUT SEX AND LOVE

One day in a workshop I was reflecting on sex and love and I had a great breakthrough. I realized that in the past, sex had left me feeling clingy and needy, disconnected rather than closer with my partner. I felt shame about my body and fearful of abandonment by my partner. That fear of abandonment made me create a "try hard to please" attitude, in which I worked hard to please and fulfill my partner sexually. I realized that these great efforts left me feeling lifeless and dull, exhausted, bored, and scared during and after sex. So, for thirty-five years, though I enjoyed orgasm, I really disliked all the work that sex entailed because it was love-less and joyless with my past mates.

I realized that I needed to develop loving, alive, and joyful feelings and a deep and creative partnership with my next life partner, before developing a sexual relationship. This would be all new for me. Her expressing enthusiastic loving feelings for me, and endearing and fun words to me, before sex, would be healing and empowering. I invented the possibility of being powerful, free, expressive, peaceful, warm, fully alive, enthusiastic, and joyful—all the time, with myself, and with her.

I declared that from now on, I would follow my heart and create what is interesting to me, what matters to me, and what is most important to me, and to her, in a loving partnership. I would be amazingly alive and happy to be with her, and create with her. That would be a very different way to relate—in a state of love and creativity first, a pleasant process where sexual expression of love could then flow in a fun and most enjoyable way.

Enthusiasm = En - theos (God-Spirit-Energy)

Enthusiasm = Having God-Spirit-Energy within

Enthusiastic Love = Love-Spirit-Energy within

THE POWER OF CREATIVE, LOVING THOUGHTS

*You feel the way you do right now because of the thoughts
you are thinking at this moment.*

—DAVID D. BURNS

Each day, in our imagination, we paint pictures of our own lives with our thoughts.

Our positive thoughts are bright colors in our daily-life painting, creating a playful, enthusiastic painting.

Our negative thoughts create an intense or dark, drab, and dreary painting.

We can step back any time during the day to look at the canvas we are creating that day . . . we can see if the picture is dreary and lifeless like a dark cloud or alive with bright colors.

Our thoughts have the power to create anger and sadness or peace, love and joy, depending on what we expect to experience and what we look for in our environment and surroundings.

The choice of what we want to create and how we want our lives to be, is ours.

We can paint a new picture each day, and when things don't please us, we are free to change our painting during the day and start a new painting any time.

The present is the best time to use your imagination to create a life painting that you want, one filled with bright colors and love.

**Is there something in your life that you would like
to change today?**

1.

2.

3.

What thoughts would make your life wonderful?

1.

2.

3.

4.

TWO PAINTINGS OF LIFE	
DARK, DRAB, DREARY OR INTENSE AND CHAOTIC	**LIGHT AND LOVELY**
Hurt	Detached, compassionate, forgiving
Agitated	Peaceful, serene, calm, balanced, harmonious
Angry, cold, hurtful	Loving, warm, kind
Sad, dull	Happy, joyful, alive, enthusiastic
Rigid, stubborn	Creative
Selfish	Grateful, abundant
Greedy	Generous

The love we give . . .
Creates the life we live.
—SANDY HINDEN

CHAPTER 7

Spiritual-Universal Love

To love another person is to see the face of God.

—VICTOR HUGO, *LES MISERABLES*

THE LIFE-LOVE FORCE WITHIN

What is love? I have learned that to love is to know someone well and to act on behalf of their true well-being. You listen to their feelings nonjudgmentally and perceive the need of the other person empathically, intuitively, and clearly, and you detach from your personal desires.

If the other person is open to your support, you then see how you could act creatively to help meet his or her needs, trying to surmount obstacles that come in the way.

When you say "I love you," in a healthy way, it is really your consciousness existing in the state-of-love and willing to act from that state-of-love.

When we develop the ability to consciously enter this heart-state-of-love, we gain the ability to relate to, connect with, and do well for others. We can be in that state-of-love for ourselves also.

When you are aware that the force of life—the Life Force—is

flowing through you, and that love facilitates the growth and development of life, so much more can be created and is possible.

Miracles from the heart happen all the time when you are in the state-of-love because you are in touch with the feelings and needs of the other, and you act to help fulfill those feelings and needs. You are fully present and listen fully, seeking out what matters most, what is most important to him or her.

These are mini-miracles we can perform each day, because deeply listening empowers the people all around us. When they in turn empower us, we have an empowering relationship.

When a group of us act from the state-of-love, we have the beginning of an empowering Beloved Community.

HONORING THE DIVINITY WITHIN EACH OTHER; SEEING EACH OTHER AS THE BELOVED

Inside you, there is a "higher you," a "wise you" who can guide you, who loves you. It has been called your Spirit, your Higher Power, the Wise One Within, the Beloved. Some think it is a small piece of the Universal Spirit, a tiny piece of God inside you, the kingdom of heaven-God-love within you.

It is not the part of you that does the everyday thinking, the chattering "monkey mind," the debating mind that creates inner dialogues, doubts, drama, and dilemmas.

The Higher Self seems to be located at a central point above it all, as if in the balcony of a theatre with the vantage point of seeing everything happening on the stage. It is a silent observer and a detached witness.

There are many names for the Observer-Witness. It has been called *atman*, or seat of consciousness by some Hindus; *Ruach*, breath of life/wind by some Jews; "Christ" Spirit, or Holy Spirit by some Christians. Buddhists may describe this consciousness as "self/no self." It is a beautiful, almost indescribable, conscious part of our self. When you find this conscious presence inside you, it guides and loves you, eliminating the need for your addictions and bad habits for pain relief. It will guide and love you to a healthier, more balanced life.

> How should two people
> treat each other if they both know God?
> Like a musician touching his violin
> with utmost care to caress the final note.
>
> —HAFIZ

When you love your partner deeply, beyond sex, money, power, and the trappings of life, you can see them as an expression of the universe. Each person is made up of 15-billion-year-old carbon atoms. The carbon atoms have come alive, are now conscious of the universe, consciously choosing to be loving, forgiving, and compassionate. You are a part of the universe expressing love to another part of the universe . . . you are the universe come alive and consciously choosing to communicate with another part of the universe . . .you are the universe communicating with the universe . . . the universe communicating with itself . . . the universe making love to itself . . .

The Indian term *namaste* literally means, "I bow you." Others have expressed it spiritually to mean:

> I honor the Spirit in you, which is also in me . . .
> I honor the place in you in which the entire Universe dwells . . .
> I honor the place in you, which is of Love,
> Integrity, Wisdom and Peace . . .
> When you are in that place in you,
> and I am in that place in me, we are One . . .
> I salute the God within you . . .
> Your spirit and my spirit are ONE . . .

That which is of the Divine in me greets that
which is of the Divine in you . . .
The Divinity within me perceives and adores
the Divinity within you . . .
All that is best and highest in me greets/salutes
all that is best and highest in you . . .
I greet the God within . . .

—FROM NUMEROUS TEXTS ABOUT YOGA

The Sufi poet Hafiz in the fourteenth century expressed it this way:

The Stairway of Existence
We
Are not
In pursuit of formalities
Or fake religious
Laws,
For through the stairway of existence
We have come to God's
Door.
We are
People who need to love, because
Love is the soul's life,
Love is simply creation's greatest joy.
Through
The stairway of existence,
O, through the stairway of existence, Hafiz
Have
You now come,
Have we all now come to
The Beloved's
Door.

TRULY LOVING, HONORING, CHERISHING, AND ADORING EACH OTHER

To love someone is to see a miracle invisible to others.

—FRANÇOIS MAURIAC

In 1631 India, Shah Jahan was Emperor during the Mughal Empire's period of great prosperity. He became grief stricken when his wife Mumtaz Mahal died during the birth of their child.

The court chronicles of Shah Jahan's grief illustrate the love story traditionally held to be the inspiration for the Taj Mahal. The construction of the Taj Mahal began soon after Mumtaz's death, with the principal mausoleum completed in 1648. The surrounding buildings and garden were finished five years later. Emperor Shah Jahan himself described the Taj in these words:

Should guilty seek asylum here,
Like one pardoned, he becomes free from sin.
Should a sinner make his way to this mansion,
All his past sins are to be washed away.
The sight of this mansion creates sorrowing sighs;
And the sun and the moon shed tears from their eyes.
In this world this edifice has been made;
To display thereby the creator's glory.

Shah Jahan must have deeply valued and treasured his beloved wife. When we were young, it was easy to become infatuated by a new lover and become emotionally attached to him or her. As we grow in consciousness we learn to become more detached, in a positive sense of the word, so as to not be addicted to our partner to the point where it harms us. We learn to not become embroiled in sex too soon because sex can cloud our judgment of the character of a person.

So, as we are more conscious and wiser, how can we feel the feelings of love, as Emperor Jahan did, to the point where we cherish, honor and adore our lover? How do we go from the beginning of a relationship with its healthy detachment, when we would not be very upset if he or she left us, to the point when we really care for and want that person to be in our lives because we do love, honor, and cherish him or her? It is a gradual process of getting to know someone over time and coming to value and appreciate that person as your partner. It occurs in natural phases.

The Beginning Relationship

- Healthy detachment . . .
- Getting to know each other . . .
- Would not miss him or her very much if he or she were gone . . .

Exploring Each Other

- Exploring each other in more depth . . .
- Discovering how each other interacts with others . . .
- Discovering each other's values and character traits . . .
- Coming to value and appreciate the person for who he or she is . . .

The Deep Relationship

- **Loving:** feeling warmth when you think of him or her . . .

- **Honoring:** holding the perception of your partner as a wonderful being on a sacred journey . . .

- **Cherishing:** knowing how very special your partner is and you would miss that person greatly if he or she was gone . . .

- **Adoring:** feeling a joyful pride to be with him or her . . . saying "I love you . . . I am so proud of you" . . .

After a period of discovery of each other's true self, we see the wonderful qualities in the person as well as his or her lesser qualities, and we accept and value the person as a whole human being.

LOVE FOR NATURE AND THE COSMOS

I speak for the trees,
for the trees have no tongues.

—DR. SUESS, *THE LORAX*

I was sent photos by a friend in Australia of an annual event in Denmark, during which whales are herded into a cove where men then kill them—a man's rite of passage. I was appalled. I decided to take action on behalf of the whales to show my love for nature.

I sent the photos and a note to others who had the capacity to spread the word and take action. I was creating the Long Island Men's Center at that time, and we use the book *King, Warrior, Magician, Lover* by Robert Moore as a way for men to grow in power and maturity, in balance with nature.

From: Sanford Hinden
To: Al Gore

Dear Vice President Gore,
Please see below and attached. Please take strong action to help the whales.

Thank you,
Sandy Hinden

From: Sanford Hinden
To: Steven Rockefeller, Earth Charter

Dear Steven,
A number of years ago we were in correspondence regarding the possibility of my working for the Rockefeller Brothers Foundation. I was referred to you by my beloved mentors Barbara and Robert Muller of the United Nations University for Peace.

As one of the founders of the Earth Charter, you came to my mind at this time.

I will be sending this to Vice President Al Gore.

Please see below and attached.

I urge you to take strong action to protect the whales from being killed.

As the cofounder of the Long Island Men's Center, I know there are alternatives for men to be initiated into manhood that are respectful of nature.

Thank you,
Sandy Hinden

From: Sanford Hinden
To: Dr. Peter van den Dungen, Founder and Coordinator, International Network of Museums for Peace, Bradford, UK

Peter . . . please see below . . . can you do something?
   Please send this to the Queen of Denmark.
   This is appalling.

Sandy Hinden

From : Sanford Hinden
To: Thomas Power, Ecademy

Thomas . . . thanks for your support . . . the whale slaughter photos are horrific . . . and Denmark prides itself on being so advanced . . .
   Will send the photos to Dr. Peter van den Dungen of the International Network of Museums for Peace at Bradford University in England . . . see if he can do something . . . will copy you . . .

Sandy Hinden

From : Thomas Power
To: Sanford Hinden

So do I.
Tx

From: Sanford Hinden
To: Ed, Australia

Hi Ed . . . the Denmark whale slaughter photos were a sign of how backward and brutal we men are in terms of how we relate to life, nature, animals and each other . . . saw this and thought of you . . .

Thanking the Monkey: Rethinking the Way We Treat Animals
www.amazon.com/review/product/0061351857/ref=dp_top_cm_cr_acr_txt?%5Fencoding=UTF8&showViewpoints=1
Author Karen Dawn

I applaud your taking a stand for the whales . . . there are beautiful tracks of whale songs on one of Paul Winter's CDs . . . I brought him to the UN to do a Concert for The Earth . . . www.livingmusic.com/catalogue/categories/sea.html

Men need new rituals for helping us go through our life passages . . . in the Long Island Men's Center (see attached . . . I enclose a flyer and the minutes from our last meeting so you see how we are organizing . . .) we will be using *King, Warrior, Magician, Lover* to help us understand more . . .
www.amazon.com/review/product/0062506064/ref=dp_top_cm_cr_acr_txt?%5Fencoding=UTF8&showViewpoints=1

The core concept is that every man has varying amounts of:

King . . . the sovereign, representing the ability to bring order out of chaos, and a benevolent use of power

Warrior . . . the ability to marshal resources, have courage, bear pain, make clear choices based on facts not emotions

Magician . . . or "alchemist," concerned with knowledge and skill, and how to use it

Lover . . . emotionally connected to others, having empathy

Each one of these attributes has many good qualities; they can turn negative however, in both active and passive ways.

Let me know if you want to do more to help the whales and/or men's consciousness raising . . .

Best regards,
Sandy Hinden
Long Island, USA

Denmark: What a Shame, a Sad Shame

While it may seem unbelievable, even today Denmark continues to brutally slaughter dolphins in the Faroe Islands. A country supposedly 'civilized' and a member of the European Union. For many people this attack on life is unknown. This bloody slaughter is to teach young men the transition to adulthood. It is absolutely incredible that no one gives a shit to prevent the barbarism committed against Calderon, an intelligent dolphin who has the peculiarity of approaching people out of sheer curiosity.

Please forward this to everyone you know.

—*From an e-mail being circulated in 2009*

The e-mail to Steven Rockefeller of the Earth Charter kept bouncing back. Perhaps he had moved. Perhaps the file was too big with the photos . . . the effort would continue . . .

Divine Love

Dr. Diane Rousseau expresses divine love this way:

> Love can be understood as the source of all energy, a wave or frequency of a pure feeling within a cultured heart. With love, we know what is needed for another, how to help or inspire and how to give.
>
> Love expands in action; a person that places love first puts the good in life above small self interests and receives more love by the act of giving.
>
> Coming from love, life is lived spiritually; the mind is engaged in day-to-day activities and functions in a positive way . . .
>
> Spirituality can be seen as the art of living love . . . love becomes the foundation of life.
>
> Religion and Faith can be understood as a reflection of one's inner love and their love affair with the Almighty, this then gives greater insight to the fundamental Laws of Life and Truth or Cause and Effect.
>
> Maintaining happiness depends on pure love and an integrated positive attitude of the mind in union with the body, heart and soul.
>
> For every action of selfless love, there is a release of stagnate energy that was stored in the cells of the body.
>
> Selfless love can heal; it creates an opening of one's Self or Spirit, direct to the unlimited reservoir of the Divine.
>
> Divine Love is the Knower in our Spirit, which remains unaffected by outer life, the Light that dwells in the heart, intuitive knowledge, right use of energy, and inspires the mind to make better decisions.
>
> A person coming from this integrated love has the ability to pursue their dreams and enjoy life with greater energy, happiness, and health while sharing their heart with all.

Divine Love is also the Beauty of the Spirit that shines through the Soul seen in all creative reflections of beauty, in acts of kindness, in caring for others, and in appreciation.

Divine Love dwells in the heart as compassion for all life, it expands and lives in giving; it is the basis of miracles.

Divine Love actively helps the Soul have faith and believe in a better world.

Divine Love inspires the mind to create a better life and a more peaceful world.

When we realize all are a part of God—Source of All Love—all life becomes sacred.

Within all Creation is the Key to know God.

In our hearts dwells the Power of Divine Love; we can heal ourselves and through this Love, change the world.

Others on the spiritual path have expressed love this way:

Love is a healing power. Love opens all doors.
Love is an ever-ready Universal Power
That's here to help us overcome
every challenge in our lives.
When we open our hearts and let love flow in,
we feel a Oneness with the Power that created us all.

—LOUISE L. HAY

There is a light
that shines beyond all things on earth,
beyond the highest, the very highest heavens.
This is the light that shines in your heart.

—CHANDOGYA UPANISHAD

Love is a powerful force. When mobilized it is strong. All the wise people on earth have known this for centuries. We are in a race to save the earth through love. Hatred is all around us, yet we have the power to restore our health and balance through love. Teach love, preach love, be love, share love, work with love, create with love, dance, sing, and paint with love. Create your business with love. Heal you community with love. Do all with love. Praise others with love.

IN THE BEGINNING were the Instructions . . .
The Instructions was to live in a good way
and be respectful to everybody and everything.

—Vickie Downey, Tewa/Tesuque Pueblo

A long time ago, in the beginning,
the Creator gave to all people and to all things
the Wisdom and the knowledge of how
to live in harmony.

Some tribes call these teachings the original Instructions,
the original teachings, or the Great Laws.

All of Nature still lives and survives according to
these teachings.

In modern times, human beings are searching
for the Instructions.

Many churches claim they have these Instructions.
Where are these teachings?

The Instructions are written in our hearts.

Great Spirit, today, whisper to me the secrets
of the original Instructions.

—Elders Meditation

When my father and teacher Rav Berg
makes a blessing over wine, he takes a long pause and
meditates on the words, to activate the Creator within . . .
The Light of the Creator is a force of unconditional love . . .
Every time we act from a place of genuine caring and concern,
we activate that force inside . . .
Today, make the decision to love everyone unconditionally.
Look at their best parts and focus only on that.
Truly love them and pay attention to the results in your day.

—YEHUDA BERG, THE KABALAH CENTRE INTERNATIONAL

Today, what is important for us is to realize
that the old sacred ways are correct,
and that if we do not follow them we will be lost
and without a guide.

—THOMAS YELLOWTAIL, CROW TRIBE

A long time ago,
the Creator gave to the people all the knowledge
on how we should live and conduct ourselves.
The Native people have been influenced by
outside 'tribes' who don't know about the Sacred Way.
Our Elders still know about the old sacred ways.
We need to consult and talk to them before it's too late.
Every family needs to seriously evaluate whether
they are living according to the old knowledge.
If we are faultfinding, putting one another down,
being selfish, being violent to our spouses or children,
if we are cheating and being dishonest,
then we are not living the old Sacred Way.

The old way is about respect, love, forgiveness and sharing.

—ELDER'S MEDITATION

A Practice for Living Well

Daily

- **Mindful, grateful, reverent**—each day, be mindful, grateful and have reverence for each other and life.

- **Sacred in the ordinary**—each day, be aware of the sacred in ordinary activities.

- **Heart connections**—allow increased heart connections to yourself, others, your communities, the planet, and the divine.

- **Acceptance and appreciation**—have acceptance, appreciation, and love for yourself and others.

- **Delight**—delight in who you are and what you do. Delight in others' being and doings.

- **Sacred moment of now**—return anytime to the sacred universe, the sacred moment, the sacred heart of love.

Weekly

- **One love**—be mindful of sacred me, sacred you, sacred us, sacred one love.

Monthly

- **Fully you**—be re-committed to being fully awake, alive, enthusiastic, expressive, and creative.

Seasonally

- **Nature's cycles**—attune to the cycles of nature, realizing that nature, universe, and creation is our source. Be grateful for your blessings.

- **Sacred transformational space**—create a safe and nurturing environment for increasing your awareness and self-discovery.

Share your thoughts, feelings, sufferings, grief, tears, joys, laughter, visualizations, art, poetry, music, and movement for creative transformation and renewal.

- **Stages of life**—explore possibilities for the stage of life you are in and how you can be more powerful and loving on life's stage.

- **Sacred ceremonies**—create ceremonies that move, touch, and inspire you and deepen your access to the sacred.

Annually

- **Passages and transitions**—honor and celebrate your life passages and transitions with understanding, compassion and forgiveness, a deep sense of reverence, and creative expression.

- **Heartful intention**—listen to your heart and mindfully gain a clear sense of direction and purpose as you are empowered to create your intention.

- **Transformational power of love**—recognize that the only transformation power to heal the hurts of all the people in the world is loving-kindness, forgiveness, and compassion.

AGAPE—LOVE FOR THE CREATOR-CREATION

The day will come when,
after harnessing space,
the winds, the tides, gravitation,
we shall harness for God the energies of love.
And on that day,
for the second time in the history of the world,
humankind will have discovered fire.

—TEILHARD DE CHARDIN

Relatedness and Interconnectedness to All Life

We share life on our planet . . .
we feel connected to a tree . . .
the majestic mountains, the singing birds . . .

We are part of the web of
connection to all things and everyone . . .

We have the power to create or destroy . . .
We need to take time to think out our choices
to be more conscious and responsible . . .

If we think in our limited way that the planet is here
to serve OUR needs, OUR wants, OUR plans only,
then we are destined to destroy it,
and we too will be destroyed . . .

Our neighbors extend globally,
not just next door to our physical house.
Every worm, bird, insect plays as powerful a role
in keeping the planet we all share dynamically alive
and running in a holistic, homeostatic way . . .

Live simply so that others may simply live
needs to become our affirmation.
Tread lightly on this planet
because it is our home
—all of our homes.

—PAULA TEPEDINO

The interchangeability of matter and spirit means the
starlit magic of the outermost life of our universe becomes
the soul-light magic of the innermost life of our self.
The energy of the stars becomes us.
We become the energy of the stars.
Stardust and spirit unite and we begin:
One with the universe. Whole and holy.

—DENNIS J. KUCINICH

Without love there is no life.

—MAHATMA GANDHI

We are both microscopic and immense. We are only one human being among 7 billion people on earth. Our earth is only a tiny planet in a galaxy of billions of stars, amongst billions of galaxies, in an expanding universe—we are so minute. Yet, we have immense power to visualize, to imagine the entirety of the cosmos.

We could live in this world more peaceably and lovingly if our spirituality were to come from recognizing the cosmic infinity and appreciating the magnificent world around us, appreciating its depth, the inner divinity of each of us, and the gift of living on one of the most beautiful planets in the universe. We are love, on this beautiful planet. It is our world to recreate—in sustainable, loving, creative villages all around the world. Ours is a sacred journey of creating a world that is loving for all.

It is with reverent appreciation and affection
for the creation-creator that we gratefully continue
our daily sacred journey . . .

Through making our inner world sacred,
we awaken to the sacredness in each other,
the sacred world of nature we live in,
and the sacredness of this blessed, vast, powerful universe.
This universe, flowing though us, gives birth to life,
wisdom, and finally, to love. . . .

HIGHER SELF DEVELOPMENT: MEDITATION AND THE EXPERIENCE OF CONSCIOUS-WISDOM-LOVE

Throughout the world, there have been many religions and spiritual traditions that can help people learn to access a higher, interior part of themselves,

The Higher Self is a realm in which our more highly evolved

expressions are formed. Altruistic love, goodwill, artistic, and scientific inspiration, philosophic and spiritual insight, the drive toward purpose and meaning in life, and humanitarian action to improve the community and the world is formed in the Higher Self. This Higher Self can ultimately attain what has been called *cosmic consciousness,* an awareness that we are one with the universe. In this state one can attain a transcendent, universal, unconditional love by letting go of fear, anger, and resentment and experiencing forgiveness, compassion, loving-kindness, and reverence for life.

Beyond the rational-debating-worried-conflict mind we have a higher mind—a conscious-wisdom-love mind that can give birth to a wonderful sense of calm and tranquility, transcendence, peak experiences, spiritual insights, expanded knowing, creative breakthroughs, innovations, and higher qualities. This conscious-wisdom-love mind is a part of being human that can be cultivated.

By taking ten minutes a day or more to develop, access, and interact with this conscious-wisdom-love mind we can create life-changing experiences that will result in emotional, behavioral and quality of life enhancements and significant relationship improvements.

Throughout the world, our religious, spiritual, and philosophical traditions have many stories of this conscious-wisdom-love mind and have called it by many names, such as the Source, the Kingdom of Heaven within, the Kingdom of God within, Holy Spirit, Great Spirit, the Muse, Guardian Angel, Higher Power, the Soul, the Still Voice Within, the Self, Higher Self, Illumination, Higher Consciousness, Inner Guidance, Inner Teacher, the Wise One within, the Light of Intuition, the Evolutionary Aspect of the Brain. Through practicing meditation and cultivating your imagination, you can shift your awareness and choices to this great part of your inner being. This cultivation of the Higher Being is the pathway for transformation of the earth into a loving planet.

God, from a kabbalist's perspective, is not a bearded man on a mountain top or a judgmental omnipotent being, but it's a force of sharing and concern and love. When you quiet down your thoughts and step away from your feelings—and just radiate concern for others—you attain affinity with God. And the moment you create this connection, you are tapping into this force. This is where fulfillment comes from. That's why love thy neighbor was the revelation of a technology, not a moral ideal! Today, be God. Be thoughtful of what others are going through. Be happy for others' happiness. Be kind to people for no good reason. Be the creative force you can be. Everything else will take care of itself.

—Yehuda Berg

When we love something it is of value to us,
and when something is of value to us we spend time with it,
time enjoying it and time taking care of it.

—M. SCOTT PECK

I feel that the essence of spiritual practice is your attitude toward others. When you have a pure, sincere motivation, then you have right attitude toward others based on kindness, compassion, love and respect. When we feel love and kindness towards others, it not only makes others feel loved and cared for, but it helps us also to develop inner happiness and peace. And there are ways in which we can consciously work to develop feelings of love and kindness. The realization that we are all basically the same human beings who seek happiness and try to avoid suffering is very helpful in developing a sense of brotherhood and sisterhood; a warm feeling of love and compassion for others.

—Dalai Lama

The astrolabe of the mysteries of God is Love.

—JALAL-UDDIN RUMI

The most important aspect of love is not in giving or the receiving: it's in the being. When I need love from others, or need to give love to others, I'm caught in an unstable situation. Being in love, rather than giving or taking love, is the only thing that provides stability. Being in love means seeing the Beloved all around me.

—Ram Dass

Eventually you will come to understand
that love heals everything, and love is all there is.

—GARY ZUKAV

Every instant that the sun is risen,
if I stand in the temple, or on a balcony,
in the hot fields, or in a walled garden,
my own Lord is making love with me.

—KABIR

He that loveth not, knoweth not God;
for God is Love.

—I JOHN: 4

What is love? Gratitude. . . .

—JALAL-UDDIN RUMI

Don't ask what love can make or do.
Look at the colors of the world.
The riverwater moving in all rivers at once. . . .

—JALAL-UDDIN RUMI

Ultimately love is everything.

—M. SCOTT PECK

CHAPTER 8

The Transformational Love Process

This is how planet Earth will be transformed . . .
it can be done easily once you learn to do it . . .
it is very simple . . . it is free . . .

In every new moment that arises in your life
*you make a **Love Choice** . . .*
you choose to treat yourself and others not with judgment,
but rather with love, compassion, and forgiveness.

Planet Earth is in transition, hopefully in a transformation from being a planet ruled by violent power and a greed-filled heart to one of loving-kindness. What will happen depends on the actions we will take to bring about more love on this planet. Only by creating sustainable, creative loving families and communities can we turn things around.

FROM AL QAEDA TO LOVE

I was on a global interactive networking website called Ecademy (www.ecademy.com) where people from around the world contact each other to do business. A young investigative journalist,

Mr. Sajid Hussain, PhD, from Pakistan, contacted me. I wrote back to him:

Hi Sajid,

I have a good story for you . . . the idea was posted on my website: What are the grievances of Al Qaeda? Do they have any just grievances that could have been expressed through nonviolent social change? In my book, *7 Keys to Love*, there is a chapter on Gandhi's and Martin Luther King's nonviolent social change movements.

Question: What prevented Al Qaeda from engaging in nonviolent, peaceful social protest and social change efforts to end the eighty-year military occupation of the Mideast, and its oil exploitation by western powers, as expressed by Al Qaeda in the Fatwah against Americans? (http://pentagonmeditationclub.org/ContraFatwa.htm)

Answer: Lack of training in:
- Personal transformation (www.landmarkeducation.com)
- Nonviolent communication (www.cnvc.org)
- Nonviolent social change (www.gamalielfoundation.org)

Solution: The peace, love, and justice movement in the Mideast is very weak and in need of resources for training the populations in peaceful, loving, social change philosophy and methods (theory and practice). Funding for global transformation is needed for peaceful, global change that includes justice and sustainable development. We need training in peaceful, sustainable global transformation that will prevent the need for global war.

Sanford

Sajid Hussain responded with this:

Thanks Sir,

I am an "investigative journalist" from Pakistan
and have extensive experience of working in the
investigative field against, all anti peace networks,
evils.

Basically, I am A PEACE PROMOTER and love to
create PEACE BUILDING MEASURES.

What . . . Al Qaeda, all those involved in crimes, evils,
rogues are gathered and unite in the platform of Al
Qaeda, these notorious gangs have made the life
miserable and painful for the innocent peoples of
the world,

If you want changes in the system, than there are
many positive and non-violent ways to convince
anyone, but if you are becoming the part of pain to
getting rights, it is never accepted in any state
any religion or society.

Dear Sir, I hope you got my point of view, anyway
please let me know how to keep in touch for future
assistance.

Hope to hear your kind reply,

Sajid

And I wrote back to him with the following:

Hi Sajid,

I have studied the human mind and heart for the past forty years . . . this is what I have discovered . . . "Hurt people, hurt people."

You mentioned that " . . .all those involved in crimes, evils, rogues are gathered and unite in the platform of Al Qaeda, these notorious gangs have made the life miserable and painful for the innocent peoples of the world. . . ."

The question is WHY do they do that?

What global conditions are producing so many unloving, brutal men and women? (mostly men)

Please see below. I have started **The Long Island Men's Center** and am willing to help men around the world start men's centers to address men's problems.

We seem to be in a global epidemic of hatred and greed. I said at the United Nations Interfaith Conference for Peace, in New York City, June 2005:

"Unless men are helped to gain legitimate work to have a family and better lives, they will be prone to being drawn into gangs, organized crime, selling drugs and guns, militias and terrorist groups that commit selfish acts and violence."

Best wishes,
Sandy Hinden

With that correspondence, I included the information on the following pages about the Long Island Men's Center.

The Long Island Men's Center

To prevent men from being drawn into negative activity we need men's groups to help men mature in a positive, constructive, empowering, loving way. Here are the purposes of the Long Island Men's Center.

Men's Centers

♪ To develop three Men's Centers on Long Island in Nassau County, Western Suffolk and Eastern Suffolk, New York for meetings and program development.

♪ To hold monthly meetings.

♪ To hold an annual retreat—the Long Island Men's Gathering (LI-MEGA).

♪ To provide programs, seminars, and workshops.

Men's Health and Wellness

♪ To help men learn relationships skills to form and stay in a healthy, loving, long-term committed relationship or marriage.

♪ To provide training in communication and social skills.

♪ To facilitate a Long Island Network to help men access positive health and human services, education, and social, cultural, and economic resources to help men meet their needs.

Values Clarification and Character Development

♪ To help men understand the values operating in their choices and their relationships at home, in the workplace, and in the community.

♪ To support men's transition to be the best they can be through helping men of all ages develop a better life for themselves, their family, their community, and the world.

❧ To help men be more collaborative with other men and women in teams.

❧ To help men learn to stop going it alone and isolating, and be more collaborative and supportive of each other in reaching personal, team, and community goals.

❧ To bring to awareness to men that when they are trained to only be strong, tough, and competitive, it can lead to domestic violence by men unable to understand and control their emotions and behavior and resolve conflict peacefully.

❧ To study and practice mutual empowerment, conflict resolution and the Seven Habits of Highly Effective People.

Work and Financial Development

❧ To help men with financial knowledge and their money issues so they don't feel shame when they are not earning enough money and turn to less than ethical behavior to make ends meet or to keep up a successful image.

❧ To provide programs on Ethical Financial Development and Entrepreneurship.

❧ To start and facilitate the management of businesses to help hard-to-employ men, including formerly incarcerated men.

❧ To help provide affordable housing for men in need of shelter.

Providing Constructive Alternatives for Youth Instead of Gangs

❧ To encourage character development and positive alternatives for youth.

❧ To provide trips to sports and cultural events.

❧ To provide programs where young men can participate in discussing concerns and issues that affect their lives.

- To help young men have positive experiences in problem solving, decision making, goal setting, planning, and implementing their action plans.
- To help young men plan and implement a community project.
- To provide opportunities for community service and mentoring.

Re-Entry of Formerly Incarcerated Men into Society

- To show men the link between childhood abuse and crime through the fact that 94 percent of men in prison were abused as children or witnessed violence or abuse.
- To point out to men that men commit the vast majority of criminal activity in organized crime, drug sales, weapons trafficking, violence, or robbery, and only boys commit school shootings.
- To help formerly incarcerated men adjust to community life and find employment.
- To encourage formerly incarcerated men to develop a strong Positive Mental Attitude (PMA).

Consciousness Raising, Communication, and Relationship Skills

- To raise men's consciousness about the power of self-image and the many negative images of men that exist in our society and media that show men as overbearing, selfish, or prone to doing harm to youth, women, and other men.
- To explore positive self-image for men and learn to appreciate men's good qualities and improve what needs to be improved.
- To provide men of all ages with opportunities to share their personal experiences and gain understanding and wisdom from each other to deepen and enrich their connection to life and become a man of wisdom, ethics, heart, and courage for the good of all.

🌢 To provide men of all ages with opportunities to gain encouragement, self-esteem, positive attitude, motivation, and confidence to meet life's challenges and overcome obstacles.

POSITIVE POWER FOR MEN

Men need new rituals for helping us go through our life passages
. . . in the Long Island Men's Center we will be using a book *King, Warrior, Magician, Lover: Rediscovering the Archetypes of the Mature Masculine* by Robert Moore to help us understand more about this subject (www.amazon.com/review/product/0062506064/ref=dp_top _cm_cr_acr_txt?%5Fencoding=UTF8&showViewpoints=1).

The core concept is that every man (and woman) has varying amounts of:

King: the sovereign, representing the ability to bring order out of chaos, and a benevolent use of power

Warrior: the ability to marshal resources, have courage, bear pain, and make clear choices based on facts not emotions

Magician: or "alchemist," concerned with knowledge and skill, and how to use it

Lover: emotionally connected to others, having empathy

I had hoped this would give young investigative journalist Sajid Hussain material to work with and I would inform him of my efforts to create an online University for Love.

*What our world needs now
is love . . .*

CONSCIOUSNESS

Internal and external are ultimately one.
When you no longer perceive the world as hostile,
there is no more fear, and when there is no more fear,
you think, speak and act differently.
Love and compassion arise,
and they affect the world.

—ECKHART TOLLE

Humans can experience Seven Levels of Consciousness:

1. **Sleeping**

2. **Dreaming**

3. **Awake**—sensing, feeling, and reacting.

4. **Thinking** and **being** at the affect of one's thinking.

5. **Becoming consciously aware** of one's own existence, surroundings, sensations, emotions and thoughts.

6. **Detached observation** while noticing the contents of one's sensations, emotions, and thinking without having to react and be controlled by them.

7. **Choosing** what to focus and act on, to consciously choose and change sensations, emotions, and thoughts.

Today,
observe and simply notice anything
within you, or what shows up for you,
that is not your Higher Consciousness
of serenity, love, joy, and abundance.

Whatever insults, hurts, angers, worries,
frightens, intimidates, or saddens you,
know it is simply internal or external stimuli
blocking you from your Higher Consciousness
of serenity, love, joy, and abundance.
Just observe it. Just notice it.
Just detach from it. Let it go. Move on . . .

Refocus on Being . . .
serenity, peace, joy, love, creativity, and abundance,
and taking action to create what most matters to you.

MINDFULNESS

We gain Mindfulness when we become aware of our feeling, needs, thoughts, motivations, and actions.

In Mindfulness, we bring our awareness back from thoughts of the past, the future, internal fantasy, or stimuli around us to be in the present moment with whomever or whatever is in front of us.

In Mindfulness, in the present moment, we practice seeing what is happening inside us and outside us. We see that internally, our mind is continually chattering with commentary or judgment. We notice that the mind is continually making commentary and we carefully observe our thoughts—just notice them without running away from them or judging them. In Mindfulness "thoughts are just thoughts." We take the emotional charge of hurt, fear, anger, or sadness out of the thought. We see that the thought is not absolute truth or complete reality, and we are free to release the thought and just "let it go" . . . detaching from it like letting a cloud drift away in the sky . . . we return to the present moment . . . we let go of all painful, hurtful, unhealthy, and unproductive thoughts. In Mindfulness, we are free to observe life without being caught in the mind's chattering and judgmental commentary.

Inside us, there can be many voices or messages that speak to us from the "committee" of people and characters in our past that we have encountered, introjected, absorbed, or taken on. The ideas of parents, siblings, other family members, teachers, authority figures, and the media have seeped into our mind and imbedded themselves there as our cast of characters.

In Mindfulness, we become aware that the messages we hear from these "committee members" as we "think" are probably not fully accurate or helpful; that they are interpretations, distortions, or departures from reality and what is really going on.

As we learn to closely observe our inner thoughts, emotions, feelings, and sensations, we awaken to the realization that happiness is not only a feeling brought on by a change in outer circumstances. We learn that happiness can start by loosening and releasing attachment to our thoughts and scripts of reality and how things have to be. When we release our "must haves," "should haves," and "ought to haves"—our expectations and demands—we are free to act on our healthy preferences and choices without attachment to outcomes.

When we release our automatic reactions to pleasant and unpleasant situations or feelings, we are free to choose what will be good for us in the long-run and not be drawn into habits of immediate, impulsive gratification around sex, money, power, substances, situations, people, places, and things.

Mindfulness can be practiced in meditation sessions or done at any time—when you are sitting, walking, standing, waiting on line in the supermarket, on the subway, in an airport, or in nature.

- Simply become aware.
- Focus on the breath.
- Bring the mind to focus on what is happening in the present moment.
- Simply notice the mind's commentary and judgments.

While walking in nature, you can become mindful of the sound of the wind in the trees, the beauty of the sky, the gentle or powerful flow of the water.

While in the home, you can notice the feeling of soapy water while doing dishes or the feeling of spaciousness after cleaning and straightening things out.

In the workplace, you can peacefully breathe and simply notice workers concentrating, the list of the things you need to do, and the important goals that need your attention.

You can also be mindful of your inner commentary:

- "I wish I could be in nature more often."
- "Vacuuming is so annoying."
- "Jim is such a jerk, I can't stand it when he yells. If he would only stop yelling, the office would run better."

Just notice your mind's commentary. You now have the freedom to not be attached to those thoughts. You can disengage from the perceptions and judgments. **Think of any activity as an opportunity to gain Mindfulness. It is a conscious-moving form of meditation that is possible almost anywhere.**

You can practice Mindfulness in meditation sessions or throughout the day using designated environmental cues that make Mindfulness essentially continuous, such as crossing the threshold of doors, hearing hourly chimes of clocks, or stopping for red lights and stop signs. Mindfulness can be as simple as focusing on three successive breaths.

At any time,
you can choose to mindfully return
to unconditional compassion and love . . .

HEALING THE HEART THROUGH ACCEPTANCE, COMPASSION, FORGIVENESS, AND LETTING GO OF THE PAST

Every day is an opportunity to mindfully practice compassion and forgiveness—for each other and ourselves. People mess up every day. We misinterpret something they say, then we believe our interpretation, then we doubt them, then we accuse them of doing something they never did. Did that ever happen to you? It happened to me. And it hurt my relationship.

Love and doubt have never been on speaking terms.
—KAHLIL GIBRAN

When someone doubts you, do you feel hurt? Do you hold that hurt? Are you unable to let it go, unable to forgive?

How good are you at forgiving? You can't be in a lasting, healthy, loving relationship unless you are able to forgive. If you can't forgive, you may carry anger, resentment, and even animosity around with you. If you do, you can't feel peace, love, and joy.

- **Acceptance:** Accept what happened.

- **Compassion:** Have compassion for the other's wrong thinking and foolish or hurtful action.

- **Forgiveness:** Have forgiveness for the other's mistake or wrong choices.

- **Let Go:** Detach, release, let go, and move on.

- **Refocus:** Refocus on what really matters most in your life.

- **Praise people:** Catch them doing the right thing. Motivate them to do more.

To be in a healthy, loving relationship, you need to cultivate and practice acceptance, compassion, forgiveness, and releasing, letting go of what happened in the far-away or recent past, and return to the present moment to refocus on what is most important to you each day. Praise yourself and others.

BEING LOVE EACH DAY

Here is a way to make sure you stay loving and make the *choice to love* each day.

From moment to moment you can return to the *consciousness of love* within you, to your *inner place of love*—your *inner abode of love*—any moment you become conscious of it. Check in with yourself to see what is showing up for you when you are with certain people in your life. Where are you when it comes to your ability to love and be in your inner abode of love when you are with them?

THE ABILITY TO LOVE IN YOUR ABODE OF LOVE AND THE WORLD											
Hate Skills	1	2	3	4	5	6	7	8	9	10	Love Skills
Dominating and Controlling											Unconditional Love
Uncaring Disinterest											Caring Interest
Shallow Listening											Deep Listening
Apathy											Empathy
Insensitivity											Compassion
Angry Resentment											Forgiveness
Coldness											Warmth
Lack of Integrity											Integrity
Inauthenticity											Authenticity
Uncommunicative											Sharing
Harsh Brutality											Gentle Kindness
Rigid Destructiveness											Joyful Creativity
Judgmental Self-talk											Praising Self-talk

Integrity is doing
what you say you will do
and not doing
what you say you won't do . . .
It is also owning up right away
when you depart from integrity . . .

It is
not withholding
what you feel and need . . .
It is sharing
what is really going on
for you and
what you feel, value, and need
and requesting what you would like . . .

Love is considering
others' values, needs, and requests . . .
and, if you can, honoring those requests
in a way that is also healthy for you . . .

Love is also
praising, encouraging, and
empowering others
to go beyond their present
behaviors and patterns
to create what matters most to them
that would heal and fulfill them . . .

Love helps free
others' imprisoned imagination
to create a wonderful world . . .

HELPING THE WORLD THOUGH LOVE

For a moment, suspend your entire belief system.
  Believe in the possibility of a world of love . . .
  Believe that a world of love already exists . . .
  Perceive a planet of peace and love. . .

- Imagine behaving in harmonious ways all day and all night. Envision an earth of tranquility and universal love and love . . .

- Realize that our belief forms our perceptions . . . which create our choices, which define our strategies and reinforce our believed-in realities . . .

- For a moment, give up the notion of global competition . . .

- For now, see beyond the world of distrust, fear, and tension . . .

- Think of a planet of sincere, wise, concerned, committed, loving beings who praise each other . . .

- Become the spirit of conscious, loving, oneness in this moment, here and now, wherever you are . . .

- See and feel all beings, all united, flowing and transforming for good . . .

- Imagine planet Earth-Love . . .

- Hold that image in your mind and heart forever . . .

- Be the spirit of conscious, loving, oneness . . .

- Perform good works and harmonious deeds, miracles of openness and love, wherever you are . . .

SUSTAINABLE, CREATIVE, LOVING COMMUNITIES

While I was in contact with the young investigative journalist, Mr. Sajid Hussain, PhD, from Pakistan, another Ecademy member from Cypress, Texas in the United States contacted me. Leslie Chapman, an eight-year veteran of the education industry with several years of experience in tutoring and education. She was doing business as Prosperity Planners, providing money management seminars to teenagers and focused on four areas: banking and goal setting, savings, debt (good and bad), and investments. Each of her seminars is four weeks long and meets for an hour and a half each week. I replied to her with a concept I had been working on for a while and had posted on Ecademy.

The Sustainable Community Investment Company

I am very concerned about what has happened to the investment world. It is now filled with greed and deception.

The investment world is no longer about the value investing concept of holding your stocks for a while in a good company, like Warren Buffett. It is now in the hands of what I call the *Skimmers* and the *Scammers*. The *Skimmers* are the day-traders who skim the profits off commodities, the currency exchange, and hedge funds, and the *Scammers* operate in the dangerous, illusory, smoke and mirrors world of derivatives. These instant addictive, Internet traders and financial con artists are making people crazier and greedier, while the environment is deteriorating.

We need a great change—for the very same reasons I've mentioned earlier in this book:

- It took 1 million years for Earth's population of humans to reach 1 billion people . . .

- In 2010, there will be 7 billion humans and we are now adding 1 billon people every ten years . . .

- In 2050, there will be 10 to 12 billion people on Earth, depending on whether we can create sustainable villages and local prosperity, which will decrease family sizes naturally . . .

- We need development that "meets the needs of the present without compromising the ability of future generations to meet their own needs"—the Brundtland Commission's definition of sustainable development.

It is very important to build sustainable, creative, loving communities around the world for nature to be in balance again and for humanity to survive and thrive. Therefore, we need investment in sustainable communities to create:

- Sustainable water sources
- Sustainable energy sources
- Affordable green housing
- Local organic agriculture
- Local green markets
- Local schools that work
- Multipurpose community centers for recreation and health and human services

We need a new investment vehicle so people can invest in sustainable communities.

I would like to partner with you to achieve this important goal. We can invent the possibility of being both inspiring and creative in the process of collaborating to build "The Game of Sustainable Community Investment." I challenge you to join me.

We would create:

- A community investment website
- Community investment computer game
- A sustainable community investment mutual fund company

Game on?

THE UNIVERSITY FOR LOVE

Though this has been mention in the introduction, it is important to recap the flow of how I began helping people in the community over thirty years ago, after receiving a bachelor of psychology degree from Queens College, City University of New York. At that time, I quickly realized the power of love to bring people together, heal their broken hearts, and empower them. By 1976, I began researching the subject of love and compiled 800 pages of quotations and images about the many facets of love that I called *Love's Journey*. At this point in my journey of the heart, I met the extraordinary Robert Muller at a speech he gave at Fr. Thomas Berry's Riverdale Center of Religious Research in Riverdale, New York. Tom Berry, director of the graduate program in the History of Religions at Fordham University (1966–1979) was president of the American Teilhard Association (1975–1987). Preferring to be described as a cosmologist, geologian, or "Earth scholar" he advocated for deep ecology and "ecospirituality."

Robert Muller was the guest speaker on the Future of Humankind, and at that time was an Assistant Secretary-General for the United Nations, who went on to have a sixty-year career at the UN, working closely with four Secretary-Generals. Robert started twenty-two specialized UN agencies and became the cofounder, and now Chancellor Emeritus, of the UN University for Peace in Costa Rica. He became a mentor and dear friend. After he created the UN University for Peace in Costa Rica fifteen years ago, I told him that we need an International Association for the Study of Love. He wrote back saying we needed " . . . a University for Love, like the one we now have for peace." I talked to him about it and said, "Let's create it." . . . he told me in his bold voice with his Alsace-Lorraine accent, "So, go do it!!" He and his wonderful wife, Barbara Gaughen Muller, agreed to be the honorary cochairpersons of the University for Love.

Lessons from the University for Love—1998

1 In our industrial, high-tech world, we are losing the inspiration that comes from love. When we realize the *power of love* we can once again become inspired through *loving-kindness.*

2 We can stop the deterioration of the mind and heart through the precious human capacity to *cherish high ideals and to love.*

3 Our world can be transformed through the *uplifting of consciousness, character, and conduct* by focusing on the beauty and power of loving-kindness.

4 Our dependence on manipulating the external-outer world, to take action on our desire for money, and our lust for power over others and nature can give away to the *finding of fulfillment within our selves through creative simplification and our daily practice of loving-kindness.*

5 From being obsessed with attaining and maintaining profit and power, we can now *find fulfillment in inner peace and love* and then in its *expression of love and creativity in the outer world each day.*

6 When we forget to love, and turn against one another, we destroy everything that stands in our way. We destroy people, relationships, things, and nature . . . we become insensitive and brutal. It has been said that throughout the ages that "Hate does not cease by hatred at any time; hatred ceases by love." *With peace and love in our thoughts and deeds, we can first transform our inner-world, and then the outer-world of our family, work space, school, community, and world.*

7 The inner-to-outer transformation of love goes forward and then rests, then goes forward, then rest again, then goes forward on its onward and upward journey of expansion

of consciousness and good deeds. Violence and war are born in the human mind and can be replaced in the human mind with loving-kindness. Over the centuries and millennium the human species is evolving from inner fear, hatred, conflict and war *to inner-love and outer humanitarianism and philanthropy, outer-love in the world.*

In 2008, I added this eighth lesson . . .

8 When a nation attacks another nation the world must come to a halt, and not retaliate. All the nations of the world must come together in *one love force* and with *higher consciousness:*

➤ Understand the unsustainable circumstances the aggressor was experiencing prior to attacking.

➤ Understand their perceived grievances and underlying needs.

➤ Assign all necessary defensive forces to prevent further attacks.

➤ Open up a constant, persistent, powerful, and all-pervasive global dialogue of conscious, loving-kindness to engage the aggressor in sharing their grievances and needs.

➤ Keep a conscious, loving global conversation alive until all needs are addressed.

➤ Engage in a process of global reconciliation and forgiveness for the grievances, the perpetrations and the dead.

➤ Use all necessary global resources over a generation to facilitate healing of the families of the dead and injured to ameliorate denial, depression, anger, hatred, resentment, and impulses for revenge to the point of pure conscious awareness, acceptance, understanding, forgiveness, and action to create better lives for themselves, their family, community, and the world.

I wrote the "Lessons from the University for Love" in 1998, ten years before the completion of *7 Keys to Love.*

Thus, in 1976, at the age of thirty, I began compiling quotes about love. As I described above, this grew to be a collection that included over 800 pages of images from magazines and quotes from hundreds of sources. The title of the book was *Love's Journey.* My mentor, Dr. Robert Muller, sent me to his book agent, who told me it would be too expensive to publish such collection of quotes and images. The manuscript stayed in a plastic box for thirty more years as it accompanied me on my journey.

Along the way, came the idea to create an International Association for the Study of Love, with Robert raising the bar by suggesting a University for Love and urging me to create it. With the publication of *7 Keys to Love* we will be beginning the development of an online University for Love.

The letter on page 194 is from Dr. Muller, former United Nations Assistant Secretary-General and cofounder and Chancellor Emeritus of the UN University for Peace in Costa Rica, 1993.

The letter on page 195 is from love educators Joyce and Barry Vissell, also 1993.

THE BUILDING OF THE UNIVERSITY FOR LOVE

The Hall of Love

At the time of publishing of *7 Keys to Love,* the following people will be recognized and honored in the University for Love's Hall of Love for their contributions in fostering love on Planet Earth.

- **Leaders:** Moses, Lao Tzu, Siddhartha Gautama, Jesus of Nazareth, Mohammed, Mohandas Gandhi, Mother Teresa, Martin Luther King, Jr., Jimmy Carter, Nelson Mandela, Desmond Tutu, Dennis Kucinich, Thich Nhat Hanh

- **Philanthropists:** Bill Gates, Warren Buffett

- **Artist/Writer/Director/Producer:** Pablo Picasso, Georgia O'Keeffe, Faridi McFree

- **Naturalists:** John Muir, Jane Goodall, Albert Schweitzer

- **Educators/Humanitarians:** Michael Harrington, Leo Buscaglia, Barbara and Robert Muller, Marshall Rosenberg, Joyce and Barry Vissell

Collection of Love Images

UNIVERSIDAD PARA LA PAZ

CREADA POR LA ASAMBLEA GENERAL ONU. RES / 35 /55 DIC 5, 1980

X ANIVERSARIO

9 April 1993

Dear Sandy,

         Your decision to create an International
Association for the Study of Love is a splendid one. I have often
recommended something similar, as well as a University of Love, like the
one we have now. for peace. There are hosts of international associations
on any subject on Earth, except the one which is most important : love.
Check however the Yearbook of International Associations to make sure.
Read also pages 144-145 on the Einstein-Freud exchange in my book
Most of All, They Taught Me Happiness. It is an essential exchange. Please
make me one of your first members. It might also interest you that a
delivered a major speech on a Global philanthropy (love for mankind)
and gaiaphily (love for the planet) at the last world conference on
philanthropy in Miami, two years ago. I have often written about it,
including in my latest production My Testament to the United Nations,
my contribution to the 50th anniversary of the UN.

         With warmest remembrances and very best
         wishes for the success of your relentless
         initiatives for a better world,

         Robert Muller

Sandy Hinden
19 Post Street
Glen Head NY 11545 USA

In Venezuela there was a few years ago a famous Ministry of intelligence
in the government, headed by a man of the name of Machado. I heard him
speak in Tarrytown. Fabulous. We need ministries of love too in government.

" Si vis pacem, para pacem."
Tels: 49-1072 · 49-1512 · 49-1511, APARTADO138 Ciudad Colón, Costa Rica, C.A. Fax: 49-1929

NEVER GIVE UP ON OTHER PEOPLE

When we are with people who have selfish interests, ulterior
motives, and hidden agendas we may feel like giving up on them
because they are so difficult. They are often cantankerous and

The Shared Heart Foundation

A CALIFORNIA NONPROFIT PUBLIC BENEFIT CORPORATION

Founders

Joyce Vissell, RN, MS
Barry Vissell, MD

Board of Directors

Barry Vissell, MD
Joyce Vissell, RN, MS
Evan Shepherd, MRP
Berry Shepherd, PA-C
Eric Alan Braun, BSEE
Bobbi Hansen, ND, PA-C
John Hansen, MA, PhD
Tolly Burkan
Safiya Williams, MA, REV
Isaiah Williams MA, REV

Sandy Hinden
19 Post Street
Glen Head, NY 11546

18 March, 1993

Dear Sandy,

Thank you for your invitation to be on the board of directors of the **International Association for the Study of Love**. We feel this is very important — and timely — work. The planet is ready to acknowledge love as the highest force at work in all affairs of humanity. We are delighted to accept your invitation.

Yours from the heart,

Barry Vissell, MD
Joyce Vissell, RN, MS

stubbornly, and even proudly, persist in their dysfunctional hostilities. They hardly ever seem to express unconditional love, friendship, caring, and sharing. Some are brilliant, willfully independent, creative mavericks who may be terribly annoying and even obnoxious at times.

When a family member, colleague, coworker, or community member doesn't listen and change for the better, it is then easy to give up on them. So many of us may have given up on "the difficult ones," and our goodness, compassion, love, and creativity remain unshared with them.

Here is an alternative. Even when you want to give up on them, try helping them by being patient. Calm patience has power.

When someone in your life is headed in the wrong direction, stick with him or her even when others abandon them. Don't throw him or her out of your heart—keep working with them. If you can, reorient him or her, pointing the way to a better path.

If it seems like they won't listen, know that you are not wasting your time and energy. Be loving inside yourself, stay focused on taking daily action to reach your goals, but also patiently guide them when you can to their working on their most important next action.

Don't be discouraged; be strong in unconditional love and share your joy and creativity whenever possible. Gently, yet strongly, stay in your own unconditional love. When you do, you are helping to recreate life and the world anew each day . . .

The most important
thing in your life
is your daily practice
of taking a few minutes
in the morning, afternoon, and evening
to calmly re-center yourself
in unconditional love,
refocusing on what matters most to you,
and sharing your love, joy and creativity
with the others and the world.

Be in integrity,
own up to when you fall out of integrity,
take responsibility and get completion.

Act with courage and dignity;
stick to the ideals that give meaning to life.

—JAWAHARLAL NEHRU

To love is the greatest thing in life;
and it is very important to talk about love,
to feel it, to nourish it, to treasure it,
otherwise it is soon dissipated,
for the world it is very brutal.

If while you are young you don't feel love,
if you don't look with love at people, at animals, at flowers,
you will find that your life is empty;
you will be very lonely and the dark shadows of fear
will follow you always.

But in the moment you have in you heart,
this extraordinary thing called love, and feel the depth,
the delight, the ecstasy of it, you will discover
that for you the world is transformed.

—J. KRISHNAMURTI

The Power of Love

Love, I say, is the energy of life.
For life, with all its yields of joy or woe,
and hope and fear,
Is just our chance o' the prize of learning love . . .
Hath been, indeed, and is.
How love might be.

—ELIZABETH BARRETT BROWNING

The Seven Keys to Love

1. Self Love

2. Physical Love

3. Emotional Love

4. Family and Filial Love

5. Altruistic and Platonic Love

6. Creative Love

7. Spiritual-Universal Love

8. The Transformational Love Process

THE TRANSFORMATIONAL LOVE PROCESS

Overwhelmed or abused Hurt, abandoned, or love-denied Fearful Closed hearted	Powerful mind Calculating, organized, efficient, effective . . . Ego driven, self-protection Can become driven by desire for material success, selfish, closed-hearted, cold-hearted and avoiding love Narcissistic love	Conscious—Mindful Heart healing Healthy self-love Compassion Forgiveness Loving-kindness Joy Warmth Sweetness
Seeking love	Healing and overcoming denied or rejected love	Being love each day Praising others

Global—Universal Love and Unconditional Love

*I realized that all these are in the three little words
'I love you' . . .
When I think of you, I feel safe, trusting love . . .
You evoke healthy love in me . . .
You are a source of love in me . . .
I miss you and appreciate you so much . . .
and want to be near you . . .
I enjoy expressing this love to you . . .
You are my loving playfriend . . .
You are my divine, loving co-creator . . .
'I love you,'*

:) SANDY

Heartoon Affirmations
(www.heartoons.com)

*I am trusting my heart . . .
I am visualizing a new me . . .
My search for my true self is not in competition with
anyone else's—it's my own personal challenge!
Trust is the love answer . . .
Love yourself.
Remember, you create your own experiences
with your thoughts and feelings.
If love hasn't worked in the past, it's probably
because you felt unworthy of it.*

—FARIDI MCFREE, INTERFAITH MINISTER, ARTIST, AUTHOR OF
CELEBRATE YOU—SELF-HEALING THRU ART & *AFFIRMATIONS* AND
PEACE ON EARTH BEGINS WITH YOU

How can you love anyone
if you don't love yourself first?
The answer is clear. You can't!
I've had a lot of experience with love
and the most important lesson
I've always learned is self-worth and self-esteem
play the most important role in the relationship.

All you have to do is drop the barriers to love
which are fear, mistrust and cynicism.
These negative emotions prevent you
from the most exquisite joy you will ever know.

Love is a miracle and you can create miracles
in your life right now.
Attitudes, values and beliefs,
shape our perceptions and behavior.
Affirmations will help you get past
the psychological barriers of fear and
change all negative expectation into positive action
that will produce love in your life . . .
sometimes, immediately.

The power to Love
is God's greatest gift . . .
for it never will be taken
from the Blessed ones
who love.

—KAHLIL GIBRAN

all the special gifts
and powers
from God will some day
come to an
end,
but love goes
on
forever

CORINTHIANS 13

CONCLUSION

7 Keys to Love

7 Keys to Love is a path that can lead to a much richer life than money alone can ever bring. Right where you are, your heart-felt love is available inside you. You can consciously choose to share it in your expressions with your partner, your family, the community, in your daily tasks and work, your hobbies and creative pursuits, and in healing humanity, nature, and the planet as a whole.

The seven keys to love are now in your pocket. Love's door to joy and wellbeing open when you want it to, by focusing your love wherever you are—in little things and in sacred moments. It can be in a simple moment of enjoyment of food or in an audacious act of global love . . . here are a few examples:

Simple, generous love can be expressed through food. I told Edith, my neighbor, that when I go food shopping, I also go to Chef's Pizza & Restaurant in East Northport, NY. They have a fabulous business because they take so much pride in what they do and they make all kinds of wonderful Italian food, judging from the satisfied looks of their customers. Chef's also makes the most incredible whole-wheat "Lite" pizza with no cheese, using tomato sauce, zucchini, and sesame seeds on the crust. I buy one slice and have the counter person add broccoli and pieces of breaded eggplant on top. It is a complete meal, very satisfying and filling. When I happily told Edith that it is one of my favorite things in life, she sardonically laughed and said, "That is so sad . . ." I laughed too, but realized that little things can be wonderful, little, loving moments. Me, my "Lite" pizza, a little apple juice, a good book, and I am in heaven. Love's joy and well-being is present for me and my "Lite" pizza . . . because I am ever-ready for it . . .

On the other end of love spectrum, on December 25, 2007, I sent an email to the Iranian Embassy in New York City with a letter attached, addressed to the president of Iran, Mahmoud Ahmadinejad, after his controversial remarks at Columbia University in September.

It was Christmas Eve and I was listening to sacred music, inspired by the spiritual love of the symbolic birthday of the master teacher of love, Jesus.

In my letter, I asked President Ahmadinejad to travel with me, in our imagination, to another part of the universe, where the beings from other worlds were gathered in an imaginary Universal Council. There, they all spoke different languages and had different names for the universal creator, whom we symbolically represent by the word "God."

I asked President Ahmadinejad to consider joining me in calling for an end to "war and hatred in the name of religion" by accepting that all religions, anyplace in the universe, call the "universal source" by different names—that the prophets who have come in different centuries, including Mohammed, all wished us to be compassionate, forgiving, truthful, kind, loving, wise, and generous—that it is foolish to fight over different names for the source—and it is much more important to teach our children how to be compassionate, forgiving, truthful, kind, loving, wise, grateful, and generous.

I asked him to return, in our imagination, to planet Earth and walk with me and our children into a garden of peace . . . and work with me to create peace on Earth.

I e-mailed the letter to the embassy in New York. They had no phone number to follow up, but I felt I did all I could at the time. Did he ever read it? I will never know, but I am glad I can now share this imaginary journey to the Universal Council with you.

As Mahatma Gandhi said, "God has no religion" . . . but if our children learn to be compassionate, forgiving, truthful, kind, loving, wise, grateful, and generous, the source of the universe we call God, if it could, would be very happy . . .

In the Laundromat near my favorite "Lite" pizza place, I met a very funny woman. I told her I was the director of a performing arts center and worked with many great comedians, and that she was a natural comedian and could be a standup comic, as she had a very quick wit.

She told me that she was too busy . . . she was a martial arts instructor, ran a women's violence-abuse prevention program, presented antiviolence programs for youth in schools, and she worked with homeless people. She was too busy indeed.

I told her I had created the Long Island Men's Center and worked on antiviolence programs, and I asked her what she thought caused violence in men. She said a number of things were a factor, including that many boys don't have fathers who serve as good role models. They often are abused their homes and then act out that abuse.

So, to all the religious leaders of the world . . . I believe when we fight over whose religion is right we are simply acting out our original pain from being brought-up in angry, unloving house-holds and loveless communities.

As we move forward, with a billion people being added to the planet each year, it is time to bury our weapons and time to love. It is time for women to teach their sons and daughters to not harm the sons and daughters of mothers any place in the world. This was sent to me on Mother's Day from a haiku teacher here in the United States:

> *Again the women*
> *come to the fields*
> *with unkempt hair.*
>
> —Kaga no Chiyo

> *This haiku depicts women too busy in the rice fields*
> *every day to worry about the beauty of their hair.*
> *Chiyo-ni was using wordplay with the word* kami,
> *which can be read as 'hair' (as in the above translation)*
> *or as 'god/goddess.'*
>
> —feminist poems by Chiyo from *Chiyo-ni: Woman Haiku Master,*
> by Patricia Donegan and Yoshie Isibashi

> *Arise then . . . women of this day!*
> *Arise, all women who have hearts!*
>
> *From the bosom of a devastated Earth a voice goes up*
> *with our own. It says: 'Disarm! Disarm! . . .'*
>
> —Julia Ward Howe, Mother's Day Proclamation, 1870

*It is nearly 140 years since Julia Ward Howe
wrote her 'Mother's Day Proclamation,'
[www.codepink4peace.org:80/article.php?id=217]
a pacifist reaction to the carnage of the American Civil War
and the Franco-Prussian War. Howe knew then what we
know now . . . it will take women's leadership to undermine
what have become the USA's greatest exports:
Violence, Weapons, and War.*

—JODIE EVANS (WWW.COMMONDREAMS.ORG/VIEW/2009/05/07-5)

Isn't it time for fathers to learn to love their wives and children and stop harming them? When boys are young we are taught to be strong and go to war if need be. We are taught to fight. If someone threatens us and gets too close, we may strike out impulsively. As founder of a Men's Center, I learned that 94 percent of men in prison in the United States were abused or personally saw violence when they were young.

In my work for nonviolence and peace, I had to train myself to calm down and control my anger. It started with my writing this book thirty years ago, when I called it *Love's Journey*. That journey led me to the United Nations and to eventually help the U.S. Department of Peace Campaign, which led to the door of the Pentagon Mediation Club.

Sanford Hinden is a peacemaker. When he first heard about the Pentagon Meditation Club, Sandy saw an opportunity and a need to work on an international transformation project for the Club. Coming forward voluntarily with the outstretched hand of a peacemaker, he demonstrated remarkable commitment and enthusiasm, joyfully spreading information about the Pentagon Meditation Club and ideas for peacemaking.

Sandy Hinden personifies a vision of the peacemakers sculpted in two identical marble monuments. The Peacemakers Monument project was another undertaking of the PMC. One of those monuments is situated in Moscow, Russia; the other one is in the United States on the campus of Shenandoah University in Virginia. Sandy Hinden's passion is to contribute to development of organizations, groups, and projects struggling to make a difference and a better world. With his assistance the Club succeeded in expanding its outreach by establishing Peace Makers Institute, Inc. Sandy became Director for Resource Development. Today he continues to be a reliable adviser for the Club and the Institute, touching our minds and hearts as a loving partner and a true friend.

—Edward E. Winchester, C.M.,
President and Founder, Pentagon Meditation Club
(http://pentagonmeditationclub.org/)
President and Founder, PeaceMakers Institute, Inc.
(http://peacemakersinstitute.org/)

Through Ed Winchester, who was a retired Air Force Captain, a comptroller for the Pentagon, and a life-long student and teacher of meditation, I learned that all wars begin within, in the "battlefield of the mind," and I came upon two extraordinary quotes:

. . . the dangers we face are unprecedented in their complexity. Ethnic conflict and outlaw states threaten regional stability; terrorism, drugs, organized crime and proliferation of weapons of mass destruction are global concerns that transcend national borders; and environmental damage and rapid population growth undermine economic prosperity and political stability in many countries.

—*A National Security Strategy for a New Century,*
The White House, 1998

Thus, we have no choice. Population growth, weapons proliferation, and greed have led us to this point—deterioration of the biosphere and society.

I wish I could put my finger on exactly what it is that Sanford Hinden brings to a project that moves it so quickly from a banal exercise, into a valid contribution to a better world. On a number of United Nations projects we have made a point of calling upon him . . . His uncluttered vision has contributed significantly. . . . Although a personal reaction, and an instinctive one, I feel that Mr. Hinden is a person to be trusted for he has shown discretion and reliability even under extreme pressure.

—Mairuth Sarsfield, Senior Information Officer,
United Nations Environment Program

We need a new economic system based on self-love and self-care, love and care for each other, and love and care for nature.

The World Based on Fear

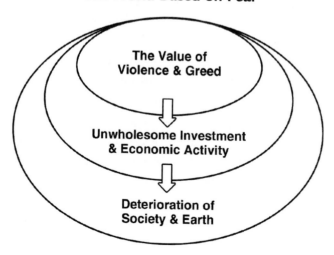

The World Based on Love

7 Keys to Love needs to be read by ministers and school teachers so they may teach parents and children about love for each other, society, and nature. It needs to be read by parents so they may create love in their homes. It needs to be read by university professors so they can instill altruistic love of the humanities, arts, and sciences in their students. It needs to be read by artists, songwriters, and musicians so they can express undying love in their works of art. It needs to be read by teachers of spiritual traditions and meditation so they can share the simply healing power of love. It needs to be read by architects and builders so the can love and preserve the earth and build in ways that foster sustainable villages and meaningful communities. *7 Keys to Love* needs to be read by leaders in business and government, who can fall prey to pressures from lobbyists or their own internal battles with arrogance and greed. They need to bolster themselves and inspire their stakeholders with the value that profit needs to be tempered with care for workers, society and nature—that to be drunk on the quest for profit leads to chaos, drama, and collapse of families, communities, and nature. *7 Keys to Love* needs to be read by entrepreneurs, who can build love into all their investment and economic strategies and activities.

The seven keys to love are now yours, to use to open the door of love to joy and well being. I wish I had found these keys earlier in my life; they would have saved me from so many mistakes. I give them to you so you can create loving relationships with your partner, your children, grandchildren, coworkers and employees, neighbors and people in your community. Love can heal and transform humanity, nature, and our planet. May the power of love be with you on your journey. And, hey—as I asked President Mahmoud Ahmadinejad—use your imagination, and I will meet you in Love's Café of the Universal Council. There we can plan the University for Love . . .

Make sure you use your seven keys... great fun, and great love will always be there for you . . .

As Neil Diamond's song said in the movie *E.T.*, we have to turn on our heartlight wherever we go for all the world to see.

Remember the scene . . . standing near the spaceship with the boy Elliott, E.T.'s heart glows . . . as he prepares to return home, Mary, Gertie, and "Keys," the government agent, show up.

E.T. says goodbye to Michael and Gertie . . .

Before entering the spaceship he tells Elliott, "I'll be right here. . ." pointing his glowing finger to Elliott's heart.

The seven keys to love will be right here too . . . when you need them . . .

Not
The End . . .

Love's Journey in the universe continues . . .

In *Love's Journey* . . . I discovered seven love keys to open the door to our heart's well-being and happiness. Along the way, I saw that our world has been created on a set of human traits or characteristics. To create a wonderful life, relationship, family, community or new world, all we have to do is teach the young to practice another set of traits. Without these traits, people cannot be happy; they just act out their daily routine of playing games with people's heads, trying to overpower them and discourage them. We can practice these positive traits and be the change we want to see in the world.

Certain things catch your eye,
but pursue only those that capture your heart.

—AN OLD NATIVE AMERICAN SAYING

PEOPLE CAN BE . . . (THE OLD WORLD)	I AM . . . (THE NEW WORLD)
Abused	Loved
Closed, Defensive	Open, Creative, Flowing
Self-Centered	Compassionate
Egotistical	Consciously Forgiving
Selfish	Generous
Insincere	Sincere
Cold	Warm
Unfriendly	Friendly
Unsupportive	Supportive
Discouraging, Judging	Encouraging, Praising
Manipulative	Co-creative
Hurtful	Kind

SEEKING WISDOM: BECOMING A SAGE . . .

What's Love Got to Do With It?

Jann E. Freed, Ph.D. is professor of business management and the Mark and Kay De Cook Endowed Chair in Character and Leadership Development at Central College in Pella, Iowa. She is also a certified Sage-ing Leader through the Sage-ing Guild (www.sage-ingguild.org). She helps leaders understand the concepts of sage-ing so they may more effectively lead quality lives.

I first met Jann through membership in the Spirit-at-Work organization. We communicated about her wisdom studies and my proposal to UNESCO, the United Nations Education, Scientific and Cultural Organization, that Wisdom Councils be created around the world to foster wise decision-making locally. Since Jan was studying wisdom (mind, consciousness, decision making) and I was writing about love (heart, feelings, emotions, compassion), I raised the question, "What is 'wise-love'?"

Jann responded with information about the process of sage-ing. She wants to prepare students to be the kind of leaders needed for the future. Her definition of a sage was adapted from the book *From Age-ing to Sage-ing: A Profound New Vision of Growing Older,* by Zalman Schachter-Shalomi and Ronald S. Miller. They define sages as people who:

- Constitute wise, prudent leadership

- Offer their experiences and wisdom for the welfare of society

- Express their hope in the future by the contributions they make for the generations that come after them

- Give generously with encouragement

- Mentor younger people who are drawn to their wisdom, and

- Model a life that finds validation, self-worth, and meaning from within.

In Jann's sage-ing research, she interview more than sixty authorities in the field of leadership ranging from Russ Ackoff to Peter Block to Max DuPree to Shoshana Zuboff, and included active and former CEOs, academics, leadership authors and consultants, and executive coaches. She focused on leaders who support creating a workplace where people are encouraged to bring their whole selves to work—their mind, body, and spirit.

From my own experience, I was aware that in the workplace, the heart, feelings, and emotions are not subjects that corporations know how to process and utilize well. Authenticity and sharing of feelings are almost taboo. We leave our feelings at the door and often pretend that undermining coworkers are not undermining us. There is lack of integrity in the workplace that most corporations can't deal with effectively. Heart healing does not take place in most work settings. Employee assistance programs are minimal, when they exist at all. Smoking for emotional calming and socializing is proliferating. Often the wrong employees are sent to "Controlling Emotions in the Workplace" workshops.

In her quest to learn more about wisdom and leadership, Jann discovered that Sage-ing is the synthesis of wisdom gained through reflecting on life experiences in order to leave a legacy for others and to live a life of purpose and meaning. It is an awakening to a *creative future* that *energizes the next stage of life.* The essence of sage-ing is based on five concepts:

- Exploring images of aging
- Engaging in life review
- Healing and repairing relationships
- Embracing one's mortality, and
- Leaving a legacy.

Jann points out that:

- Wisdom is not an automatic benefit resulting from more years of life experience.

- Becoming a sage is an intentional process based on reflection and doing the necessary "inner work" needed to pass on wisdom to others as a future legacy.

- The journey of becoming a sage is important for couples in particular to continue growing in similar directions.

- It is easy for couples to grow apart when they are not on this journey together.

- Sage-ing is living life on purpose and with passion, and for most people this is not necessarily intuitive.

- People need to make intentional choices about how they spend their time, energy, and resources.

- This requires two people to share values, goals, and dreams for the future.

- When couples are conscious about doing this inner work together, "true love" can emerge.

Jann thinks that growing in life experience together can be an *adventure of love*. She sees love as a process that emerges from real communication about creating a life that matters.

I am passionate about retiring the word "retirement" and working to create a new model of living the next phase of life.

Research indicates that for most people in the second half of life, *meaning trumps money* and *significance trumps success*.

In the end, most of us want to be reassured that our life mattered—that we made a difference in the world in some way.

The sooner we figure this out, either as an individual or as a couple, the better.

—JANN FREED

Thus, rather than couples separating because they are growing in different directions, love can continue to be refreshed and flow once again when we figure out how to fully express our values, goals, and dreams as a couple. It is essential for couples to have a midlife review to explore how they can share their visions, values, and dreams.

They can then consciously choose to support the fulfillment of each other's values and explore how to help create each other's dreams.

Love can then become part of a process of sage-ing. When conscious, wise minds are connected to compassionate loving hearts we have the flowering of wise-love.

A New Business Model for the World

As a final note, I want to encourage the work of Jann Freed to share wisdom with leaders of business and government. These leaders have become obsessed with power and money for too long, to the detriment of the environment and our communities. Selfishness and the follies and foolishness of corporate and government leaders is leading to the melting of the icecaps, which will flood port cities, beach communities, and island nations of the world.

This pending disaster may still be ameliorated and mitigated through desalinization plants and water pipelines. One solution would be to build 1,000 to 2,000 desalinization plants and water pipelines to channel water into dry interiors over turbines to gain electricity and use the water for drinking, agriculture, cooking, and sanitation.

Many leaders have become arrogant and indifferent to the needs of humanity and the Earth. Future leaders of business and government need to humble themselves as servant-leaders.

We need a business model that heals hearts and the earth.

From the Negative Power Model to the Positive Power Model

We can now consciously and compassionately recognize that humanity has been mentally trapped in the *negative, domination power model,* caught in a loop of arrogance, control, manipulation, force, violence, subjugation, exploitation, and angry rebellion.

This *million-year-old negative power model* can now be replaced with a *new conscious positive power model,* through which we can all experience inner freedom, co-empowerment, collaboration, co-creation, invention, caring, sharing, compassion, love, wisdom, humility, and high levels of productivity. We can use words to co-create the life and world we want.

Though the *negative domination power model* has existed for a million years, the choice is now ours to consciously create and practice returning to the *new conscious positive power model* each day, and help the planet transform through our conscious love.

We are at the beginning of creating a new economic system based on self-love and self care, love and care for each other, and love and care for nature. This new win-win-win business and economic model will transform the planet.

We are creating the new world by putting one foot in front of the other and being patient, empowering, and communicative, creating conversations that praise people instead of minimizing and subjugating them.

Praise frees the gifts and treasure in people to create the world we really need and want . . . a loving world in harmony with nature.

Commenting on the vagaries of Washington politics . . .

"If you want a friend in Washington,
get a dog."

—PRESIDENT HARRY TRUMAN

Why do I love my dog? They say having a dog adds several years to you life. For me, my three-and-a-half-year-old cockapoo Maggie is my fountain of youth. She makes me laugh or chuckle every day with her playful antics and loyalty. She's incredibly smart and has personality you wish most people would have. There is nothing like the unconditional love she provides. My suggestion to everyone is: get a dog, and add a new dimension of love to your life!

—Carol Bergh

Without love there is no life.

—Mahatma Gandhi

I am so small.
How can this great love be inside me?
Look at your eyes. They're small.
But they see enormous things.

—Rumi

Oh the comfort,
the inexpressible comfort
of feeling safe with a person,
having neither to weigh thoughts
nor measure words,
but pouring them all right out,
just as they are—chaff and grain together—
certain that a faithful hand
will take and sift them,
keep what is worth keeping,
and with the breath of kindness
blow the rest away."

—Elizabeth Barrett Browning

Resources

1. Self Love

Self Love Article

www.psychologytoday.com/articles/index.php?term=pto-2485.html
&fromMod=popular_depression

Compassion Quotes

http://thinkexist.com/quotations/compassion

www.finestquotes.com/select_quote-category-Compassion-page-0.htm

2. Emotional Love

Thich Nhat Hanh on Love: www.katinkahesselink.net/tibet/
Thich-Nhat-Hanh-love-q.html

Nonviolent (Compassionate) Communication: www.cnvc.org

Love Tips by Martha Baldwin Beveridge: www.lovetips.com

Love Healing by Kathryn Alice: www.kathrynalice.com

3. Physical Love

Holistic Sexuality

Intimacy Retreats:

www.intimacyretreats.com

www.intimacyretreats.com/peacefulpassion.htm

www.intimacyretreats.com/tsb.htm

The Kosher Sutra: http://browseinside.harpercollins.com/index.
aspx?isbn13=9780061668357

Treatment

Hazelden: www.hazelden.org

Gardening

Children's Mother Earth Gardens: www.worldcmeg.org

Gardens for Humanity: www.gardensforhumanity.org

4. Family Love

Leo Buscaglia: http://en.wikipedia.org/wiki/Leo_Buscaglia

Marriage & Family Therapy Associates Healing Quotes:
www.mftassociates.com/quotes.html

Families Advocating for Compassionate Treatment (FACT):
www.familiesact.org

Alanon: www.al-anon.alateen.org

5. Platonic Altruistic Love

Peace

Pasos (Steps) Peace Museum, NYC: www.pasospeacemuseum.org

International Network of Museums for Peace:
www.museumsforpeace.org/index.html

US Department of Peace Campaign: www.thepeacealliance.org

World and Earth

Whole Earth Green Group: www.eastwestnyc.com/events.html
(click on second Wednesday of the month)

Robert Muller's 5000 Ideas: www.robertmuller.org

Good Morning World: www.goodmorningworld.org

Paradise Earth: www.ParadiseEarth.us

Community

Gamaliel Foundation: www.gamaliel.org/default.htm

6. Creative Love

Creativity

Orbiting the Giant Hairball: www.lukew.com/ff/entry.asp?352

Heartoons: www.heartoons.com

Sark: www.planetsark.com

Antoine de Saint-Exupery Quotes: www.brainyquote.com/quotes/authors/a/antoine_de_saintexupery.html

7. Spiritual Love

Thomas Berry: www.thomasberry.org

Teilhard de Chardin: www.brainyquote.com/quotes/authors/p/pierre_teilhard_de_chardi.html

Mystical Love Poets

Rumi: www.poetseers.org/the_poetseers/mystic

Kabir: www.poetseers.org/the_poetseers/kabir/index_html/?searchterm=Kabir

Hafiz: www.poetseers.org/the_poetseers/hafiz/index_html/?searchterm=Hafiz

8. The Transformational Love Process

Transformation

Landmark Education: www.landmarkeducation.com

Joanna Macy: www.joannamacy.net

Pentagon Meditation Club: http://pentagonmeditationclub.org

PeaceMakers Institute, Inc.: http://peacemakersinstitute.org

Hazel Henderson: www.hazelhenderson.com

Jean Houston: www.jeanhouston.org

Index

About the Author

Sanford (Sandy) Hinden has a BA in psychology with extensive studies in human relations, group facilitation, meditation, anger management, conflict resolution, assertiveness training, co-counseling and nonviolent communication.

Sandy is a creative idea person and a high-energy, action-oriented, goal-seeking doer. He is an author, coach, workshop facilitator, public speaker, community organizer, trainer, project and program developer and consultant specializing in innovation, marketing, pubic relations, and fundraising. He has worked to create a better world for over thirty years in the arts, health and human services, for the environment and for peace, including United Nations affiliated projects and local anti-violence and development campaigns.

Sandy founded Universal Children's Gardens (1979–1985), which is now being redeveloped as Children's Mother Earth Gardens; The Concert for the Earth at the UN (1984); and WholeEarthARTS (2008). He affiliated fifty museums worldwide with the UN as the International Network of Museums for Peace (2000). Sandy was program director for Community Partners for Coordinated Services (1998–2000), bringing school and agency social workers together to help at-risk and in-need children and families for Suffolk County, New York.

He founded the Long Island Men's Center (2005), helping men access healthcare, communications and relationship skills, youth gang prevention and mentoring, prisoner re-entry into the community, and economic development. He facilitates a monthly Whole Earth Green Group at East West Living in Manhattan and is promoting global desalinization plants and water pipelines to ameliorate rising seas by using the water for electricity generation, agriculture, sanitation, cooking, and drinking.

Sandy is Executive Director of the Dix Hills Performing Arts Center and Co-Director of the John Lennon Center for Music & Technology at Five Towns College on Long Island.

As a coach and consultant, Sandy works with clients to overcome obstacles and barriers by increasing resources and expanding their community of support to create opportunities to fulfill their dreams, potential, and possibilities.

As a workshop leader and public speaker, he seeks to be creative to inspire, motivate, and empower audiences, workshop participants, clients, and coworkers.

7 Keys to Love—Opening Love's Door to Joy & Wellbeing fosters sustainable communities of wellness, love and abundance, aligned with nature.

www.sanfordhinden.com
www.7keystolove.net
www.relationshiplove.net

SANFORD HINDEN WORKSHOPS

Sandy Hinden has worked with communities locally, nationally, and globally for thirty-five years, developing organizations, programs, and projects. He is author of *7 Keys to Love,* executive director of the Dix Hills Center for the Performing Arts, and co-director of the John Lennon Center for Music & Technology at Five Towns College on Long Island, New York. Sandy is cofounder and president of the Long Island Men's Center and facilitator of the Whole Earth Green Group at East West Living in Manhattan, New York City. He has worked to create community gardens, children's gardens, tree planting, and concerts for the Earth, peace museums worldwide, and coordinated health, education, and human services for at-risk and in need children and families in Suffolk County, New York.

7 KEYS TO LOVE WORKSHOP

You will learn the seven keys to healing your heart and building your character so you can experience wellness, friendship, and joy, enabling you to lovingly create kind and fulfilling relationships with others, your family, and your community. You will explore the rooms in Life's House of Love: personal, interpersonal, familial, community, creative, for the eternal source-God, and for nature, and learn to experience and express love in all areas of your day-to-day life. In order to heal our planet, we must first heal our broken hearts and create loving, creative, sustainable families and communities. We can go beyond our present system that exploits sex and violence, produces unethical behavior, drives us to consume unnecessarily, and fosters family and community discord. We can create a sustainable social and economic system grounded in good character that exhibits self-love and self-care, love and care for others, and love and care for nature.

COUPLES COMMUNICATION WORKSHOP

Most couples go through five phases in the Couple's Journey: 1. The Honeymoon; 2. Day-to-Day Living; 3. The Power Struggle; 4. Disappointment and Major Conflict (and possible separation); and finally, if a couple works on communication, 5. Reclarification-Reconciliation-Recommitment. This workshop is for couples interested in acquiring tools and techniques to keep their love growing. Instruction includes practice of methods presented in The Johari Window of Awareness, Feedback and Sharing; The Passive, Passive-Aggressive, Aggressive, and Assertiveness Model of Communication; Compassionate Communication; and 7 Keys to Love.

Benefits for couples include transforming fights into fair, respectful disagreements, exploring possibilities and dreams, increasing understanding of feelings and needs, creating great communication and conversations, and experiencing more love and fun with each other daily.

FAMILY COMMUNICATIONS WORKSHOP
FOR PARENTS & GRANDPARENTS

The Family Communications Workshop will help parents and grandparents improve their interpersonal communication and heal all kinds of family disputes. With the absence of respectful, authentic communication, love in the family is not possible. Edward Dabrowski, Federal Director of the Shared Parenting Council of Australia (SPCA) has said, "Love is the ingredient that excites the human spirit and energizes the human being to selfless service. The gift is in the giving and in receiving. It seems that no matter what discord or dysfunction occurs, we are all clumsily striving for love, mutual connection, understanding and appreciation. Sandy, the love you have for humanity spills onto the page as wisdom and revelation." This workshop brings family members to a common consensus and instills a respectful view of each other.

SUSTAINABLE COMMUNITY DEVELOPMENT—
Bully & Gang Prevention for Schools, Organizations, and the Community

We live in an overpopulated world, where many unemployed people migrate to find work. When young men are unemployed for too long, violence can erupt in a home, school, or community. because men are brought up on fighting models; are not trained in communication; don't share their experiences of neglect, abuse, abandonment, rejection, and betrayal or their feelings of hurt, sadness, and anger; and don't seek help.

Young men can be prone to impulsive violence in conflict situations. They can become bullies and members of gangs, get drawn into selling drugs, guns, and crime, and become involved in long-term organized criminal activity.

This workshop will help schools, nonprofit organizations, and local government reach out to at-risk youth and gang members to help them get back on track. We will understand the five needs that gangs fulfill for young men and women and form a Men's Center to mentor young and older men and help youth develop character, communication skills, creative thinking, problem-solving skills, community service, and legitimate businesses. We will form an ongoing Youth and Community Partnership.

This workshop is for the whole community: school administrators, teachers, social workers, parents, legislators, nonprofit agency personnel, youth bureau directors, minority affairs officers, business persons, clergy, and police. We will align forces in the community for the good of all.

"Your workshop should be required attendance for all schools."

—Gary Rosenberg, graphic artist, book designer, and co-creator of The Jon & Jayne Doe Series.

Jon and Jayne Doe are fictional characters who represent the voices of today's teens (www.jonandjayne.com).

Helping Bullies Workshop

Bullies take on many forms in society: School-Yard Bully, Gang Leader, Overbearing Spouse, Boss-as-Petty Tyrant, Brutal Police, Jailhouse Dominator, Organized Criminal, War Lord, and National Dictator. The shaping of bullies occurs in childhood when children are taunted by adults, teenagers, or other children, are neglected, insulted, abused, rejected and/or abandoned. They have a storehouse of pain inside them. They turned mean and "hurt people, hurt people." Bullies never had peaceful, constructive, meaningful conversations when they were growing up. They never experienced empathy and positive communications skills. They never processed their original pain. Ego-inflating bullying behaviors actually serve the bully as a drug to numb their ever-present inner pain from their past.

In this workshop, you will learn to help bullies calm down, communicate assertively and respectfully, experience empathy and compassion, have meaningful conversations, and then finally, help them process their original wounding to experience the healing of the Fisher King/Queen within and the flourishing of their lives.

Five Skills Communications Workshop for Teens

In this highly interactive workshop, teens will learn to talk to each other to end physical and verbal hostilities, locally and globally. They will turn destructive put-down speech into constructive communication skills and empowering projects to better the community.

Teens will learn pro-social skills needed to succeed in the family, workplace, community, and the world: positive self-talk; The Johari Window of Awareness, Feedback and Sharing; The Passive, Passive-Aggressive, Aggressive, and Assertiveness Model of Communication; Compassionate Communication; Calming and Conflict Resolution; Public Relations Skills; and Fundraising Skills for Projects to Make a Difference. Teens will become empowering forces for good in their communities and be guided to be future leaders.

SANFORD HINDEN
www.7keystolove.net